Jon,
May this book ignite
the greatest version
of you! Thank you
for SPARKING others to
new levels.

In His grip,
Stacy Afanord

Romans 12:2

Spark

5 ESSENTIALS
TO IGNITE
THE GREATNESS
WITHIN

SPARK: Five Essentials to Ignite the Greatness Within

Published by:
Tremendous Leadership
PO Box 267
Boiling Springs, PA 17007
717-701-8159   800-233-2665
www.TremendousLeadership.com

ISBN# 978-1-949033-29-8

First Printing, June 2020

Printed in the United States of America.

Spark

5 ESSENTIALS
TO IGNITE
THE GREATNESS
WITHIN

DR. TRACEY C JONES

PREFACE

My 2019 was filled with a disproportionate share of trials and losses. And yet as the year ended, the clouds parted and I entered the next one celebrating two tremendous milestones in my personal and professional life, becoming a doctor and a wife. With all the highs and lows over the past six months, I was finally able to finish this manuscript, which I am honored you have chosen to read.

The timing of completion was providential as everything was coalescing. I could now share how I ignited my internal greatness and encourage others to do the same. After two glorious months leading into 2020, I was on top of the world spiritually, personally, relationally, professionally, and financially —and then March of 2020 hit and life as we know it was dramatically altered.

As I spent the first few weeks of my quarantine re-reading and re-editing my manuscript, I wondered if my triumphant tone would be tempered or even dosed by the unthinkable landscape that had smothered the globe. And it became more evident to me that igniting greatness is a personal mission, one that is undertaken despite the odds or external circumstances. Indeed, often when life goes awry, that's when we must go deep and find out not just what happened, but more importantly, where we want to arrive next. A crisis is often the best time to spark the change fires waiting to burn off the dregs of what was and put us on the path to our preferred future.

There is no more significant time than now to celebrate the resilient nature and adaptive capacity within each of us. We shall overcome this pandemic; it's not a question of if, but when. Humankind is remarkable in its ability to regenerate. **Sparking** your innate great is defined by attitudes and actions, not circumstances. This book provides the five essentials to navigate your way out of not just this but any crisis. As they say, when the going gets tough, the tough get going; or as I like to say, when the going gets tough, the tough get *growing*. Here's to unfolding the highest version of you!

ACKNOWLEDGEMENTS

This book is born out of my doctoral research in the Theory of Motivation. I had the two greatest readers in the world, without whom I would have never crossed the finish line. To Dr. Ken Blanchard and Dr. Kevin Gushiken, thank you for your wisdom, your encouragement, and your time in helping me build up the foundation of leadership literature and for your assistance in cultivating previously uncovered truths.

To all the supporters of my father and mother, Charles and Gloria Jones, who came alongside me when I returned to run the business, your constant encouragement and connections have allowed the Tremendous legacy to not only survive, but to thrive. And to my new tremendous tribe that has welcomed this prodi-*gal* back home after many decades, this book would not be possible without you.

Any writer knows they are only as good as their literary and editorial team. I want to thank my co-leader, Leah Hess, for keeping me on point; and to my editors Frank Steele and Tim Schulte. Your keen eye and grasp of my message took a mediocre manuscript and chiseled it into something beyond tremendous.

To the Holy Spirit, who took control of the keyboard, my mind, and even my time when there was no way I could make it all happen. Thank you for showing me that you are the source of each and every thought on the pages that follow. May your infusion of these written words **SPARK** the greatness in every person who reads this book.

TABLE OF CONTENTS

AUTHOR'S NOTE

"Many people have the ambition to succeed;
they may even have special aptitude for their job.
And yet they do not move ahead. Why? Perhaps
they think that since they can master the job,
there is no need to master themselves."

—John Stevenson

Did anyone ever tell you that you have greatness within? This fact may have never crossed your mind, you may have refused to acknowledge it, or you may have grown up with others telling you just the opposite. So many people go through life unaware or unwilling to accept the realization that they can—and will—be great. Human beings created the Seven Wonders of the World, split atoms, and ushered in the Age of Enlightenment and the Industrial Revolution. We gaze with reverence upon those who are masters of their destiny and yearn to strike out from the crowd like them. Much of our modern-day messaging, however, convinces us we are merely mediocre mice on the third rock from the sun, evolved from a cosmic explosion, eking our way through life until our time is up and back to the dustbin we go. But that simply is not true.

Our present society frowns on standing out from the crowd, as if our achievements somehow harm the opportunities available to others. For some unscientific reason, they claim if we are great, then others are lessened, weakened, or marginalized. This is nonsense. If the truth of your greatness hasn't dawned on you or if you've heard about it but haven't thought you could truly claim it, I am eternally grateful you chose to pick up and read this book because we're about crack the code on your self-awareness and self-worth. But just like everything else in life, there must be an initial **SPARK**, a point of ignition, a source of origin. Next there must be an intelligent and creative design applied to the combustion lest the forces of nature scatter you into oblivion. Lastly, there must be a continuous source of fuel, so the flame doesn't extinguish itself. Nothing in life just *happens*. There must be an action and a reaction. It's science.

Today, we hear a lot about respect. Growing up I would laugh endlessly when comedian Rodney Dangerfield would exclaim, "I don't get no respect!" Psychologists, therapists, and countless self-help books all orient the individual to a healthy grounding in self-respect. We hear the perennial self-esteem anthem from the late, great Aretha Franklin, R-E-S-P-E-C-T and are told everything hinges on our level of self-respect. I certainly agree that we must have confidence in ourselves, however, I have always been one to know how broken, pathetic, and mean-spirited I truly am. Romans 3:10 tells us, *"As it is written: 'There is no one righteous, not even one'."* Let's not forget as well, we all have a past that continually reminds us of who we are and what we are capable of. My father used to say, *"Only an honest man can be honest about how dishonest he is."* When I look in the mirror, I know what's beneath the surface. Some good, but there is plenty of bad.

I would like to offer a slight paradigm shift in this book. Rather than telling you to *respect yourself*, my goal is for you to apply the principles you read to *perfect yourself*. Now wait just a minute, I can hear it now, "Ms. Tracey, perfection is a dirty word! There are millions of recovering perfectionists that will be triggered!" One important point; there is a world of difference between being perfect and pursuing perfection. We'll never get to be perfect this side of Heaven. There will always be some character issue that needs smoothing, some blind spot that needs removing, some less than charming tendency that needs grooming. That is called growth. But in discovering and facing my imperfections, I can become a more closely aligned version of my best self. Isn't that how you go from bad to better, good to great?

Pursing perfection enables us to live a life of liberty whereby we are not bound by strictness, exactitude, or legalism. We are free to take risks, make mistakes, and be gracious with ourselves—all without engaging in self-loathing. We are to be continuously transformed, sanctified, justified, and glorified, until we finally arrive! There's an indescribable joy to life when we approach it this way. Never forget, each of us is a work in progress....so let's get to work!

I haven't had an easy life, but it has been a blessed one. This book contains a plethora of my personal pruning. The beauty of pruning is that your faith gets laid bare. I give God the thanks that I now see glimpses of how his hand was working in and through each of my successes, but most importantly my mistakes. I begin each morning reading Oswald Chambers' daily devotional, *My Utmost for His Highest*. The July 13th meditation is one I cling to:

"God has to remove our friends in order to bring Himself in their place, and that is where we faint and fail and get discouraged. In the year that the one who stood to me for all that God was, died—I gave up everything? I became ill? I got disheartened? or—I saw the Lord?"

This meditation rang true a second time in my life in October of 2019 when my mother passed on to glory. The first time was when my father passed in October of 2008. Every tragedy in life may result in transcendence. Never, ever, lose sight of that.

I'm not the smartest, the most talented, nor the most gifted gal in the world; but I probably am in the top 10 percent as far as most adaptable and most driven. I worked hard to develop my book smarts, recently completing a Ph.D. in Leadership which inspired the contents of this book. I honed my street smarts by diving into every professional challenge I could find across the globe, from going to war as an officer in the military, to experiencing the intense pace of the tech industry, only to finally land in the world of small business and entrepreneurship. I love change, I love learning, and I love leading. However, I was having to repeat too many lessons, too many times and felt like the next breakthrough was always just beyond my reach and worse yet, capability.

After decade upon decade of working with people, gathering different experiences, and getting a better understanding of myself, I've discovered the most important aspect in **Sparking** greatness is my spiritual smarts. I was taught this truth from a very early age but never claimed it for myself. I grew up in the world of standardized testing and knew the value assigned to a person's IQ. Test scores matter. They get you into competitive schools and choice fields of employment. Today, much of the management research and literature focuses on the softer side of leadership—commonly referred to as Emotional Intelligence—or EQ. Relationships matter because you can't lead people if they won't follow. If you don't have authentic followers you are not a true leader. IQ and EQ are essential ingredients to creating the best version of you. This book, however, is going to weave in the final piece of the trifecta—the Spiritual Quotient, or SQ. We truly are body, mind, and spirit, and it takes all three coming together in unison to ignite the greatness within.

When writing the final dissertation to finish a doctoral program, you are required to disclose your researcher bias. No matter how objective we try to be, or think we are, we are a product of our DNA, our upbringing, and our experiences. That's not a *bad* thing—but it is *some* thing. I value understanding where someone is coming from because that helps provide the context for where they are going to take me. All of us who love personal development are researchers. Researchers interpret the world through a personal and previously conceived conceptual lens.[1]

No one has lived your life but you. That's why it's important not to erroneously judge others' experiences through your own lens. There's an adage about walking in someone's shoes—meaning we need to take time to understand another's path because each of us is on a singularly unique life journey. There are some commonalities across humanity, but how we process events is what makes us unique individuals. The truths I am going to share in this book are timeless and universal. They apply to every single person. There is great diversity in the body, however there is also immutable unity. We were created as a collective and working, living, and playing together is how we function best.

The Imago Dei

As a believer in Jesus Christ and a daughter of God, I have claimed my spiritual inheritance, meaning that my DNA isn't just cells and synapses. DNA is the Divine Nature's Autograph. That's right. The *imago dei*, the image of God, is imprinted into every being whether we chose to acknowledge it or not. But hey, who wouldn't want to claim a direct descendance from the creator of the cosmos? Television superstar Judge Judy asks her plaintiffs who they want to hitch their star to. By now, you have probably figured out my answer to that question.

The concept of the *imago dei* is rooted in the biblical truth that every individual is created in the image of God and gifted with divine aspects manifested through the ministry of the Holy Spirit. The first appearance of the Holy Spirit in the Old Testament was in a creating role (Gen. 1:2). When we engage in self-loathing or doubt, we are insulting God. Oswald Chambers wrote, *"The way we continually talk about our own inability is an insult to the Creator."*

To say that humans are in the image of God is to recognize the special qualities of human nature which allow God to be made manifest in humans. In other words, for humans to have the conscious recognition of their being in the image of God means that they are the creature through whom God's plans and purposes can be made known and actualized; humans, in this way, are co-creators with God. Do you see yourself as a tool that is ready and willing to be used by the Holy Spirit? Do you know the kind of power you have at your disposal? Have you embraced and claimed it, and do you pour it out on a daily, or even hourly, basis? Like anything else in life, if you don't use it you will lose it. It is a universal truth that the God seed only becomes active when you tend to it.

Because I am a believer, I have the gift of the Holy Spirit at work within me in the here and now, in addition to eternal life (as if that weren't enough). I would be remiss if I did not explain the most important gift of all and that is the transformation of self-efficacy (earthly motivation) into spiritual efficacy (eternal motivation). I have committed my life to the pursuit of mortal revelation, but true greatness becomes possible when we infuse this pursuit with daily doses of divine inspiration.

Intentionality Trumps Capability Every Time

A life transformed by grace equates to a life poured out in deeds. The goal in igniting our inner greatness is not to boast or earn a living, recognition, or even salvation, but to reflect grace. They say you must be willing *and* able to achieve anything. I wholeheartedly agree with this statement. However, I'd go even further. You can't just be willing *and* able, but you must be willing, able, *and* EAGER, because without enthusiastically adding combustion to fire you into action you'll never turn your internal gyros over and gain traction. Life has too many obstacles to overcome without a well-tuned intrinsic motivational motor in overdrive.

It took me many years to understand that you can have capability, but without intentionality you're dead in the water. For example, there were many things in my life that I wasn't sure I could pull off. But I sure knew I would try my best. If I didn't, I'd have to live with regret and that is so much more painful to me than failure.

I can give you all the tools, support, money, hugs, or affirmation in the world but if you don't want to put them to use in your life to affect change it's all a waste. This failure to launch is not on those trying to help you—it's on you.

Read the Vision of the Valley of the Dry Bones in Ezekiel 37. This chapter recounts the prophet Ezekiel's prophecy of the restoration of Israel, a seemingly impossible task due to Israel's division and dispersion. Ezekiel was to tell the bones that God would make breath enter the bones and they would come to life, just as in the creation of man when God breathed life into Adam (Gen. 2:7). Ezekiel obeyed, the bones came together, flesh developed, skin covered the flesh, breath entered the bodies, and they stood up in a vast army.

Do you want your dry bones to live? Then be encouraged and read on, because the best is yet to come!

INTRODUCTION

A group of junior-level executives were participating in a management training program. The seminar leader pounded home his point about the need to make decisions and act on these decisions.
"For instance," he said, "if you had five frogs on a log and three of them decided to jump, how many frogs would you have left on the log?"
The answers from the group were unanimous: "Two."
"Wrong," replied the speaker, "there would still be five because there is a difference between deciding to jump and jumping."

If you laughed at this story, this book is for you! If you took offense, please step away from the page and put this book down. Seriously though, most of you subconsciously realize by this stage in life that there truly is a world of difference between capability and intentionality. I can remember as a younger leader being taught, if I just give people enough training and get out of their way, they'll amaze me! Hogwash. A few will; most won't. That's because for all the training in the world, we never teach people that the only form of motivation is self-motivation. You may have witnessed friends or loved ones struggling who desperately needed to make changes, only to remain stuck in the sands of self-pity. Or you may have wondered why you can't seem to get the traction you so desire. In this book I share the tools to help you bridge that gap. Tools are important. But do you know what's more important than tools? Picking them up and putting them to use. But in order for you to begin swinging the hammer with power, like Thor, you'll need a source of ignition…..a **SPARK**.

If It's to Be, It's Up to Me

You alone have the keys to unlock your potential. Whether you will or will not is dependent on something called, personal agency. Personal agency is the act of deliberately or intentionally exerting positive influence.[1] Personal agency refers to your capability to originate and direct actions for given purposes. An individual's degree of agency is influenced by the belief in their effectiveness in performing specific tasks—also termed self-efficacy—as well as by their actual skill.[2] Hence, we see the link between capability (actual skill) and intentionality (potential skill). Another term researcher's use to describe personal agency is motivation. Motivation is defined by social cognitive researchers as a process in which goal-directed behavior is instigated and sustained.[3]

The Perception of Self (It Really is All About You)

The key tenant of self-efficacy is found in the word "self". Self-efficacy theory is rooted in the perception the individual holds regarding their own level of performance, as well as development. In essence, life is not about how others view you as much as how you view yourself. The theory of self is what causes each person to feel, think, and act in particular ways. Self-concept refers to a generalized self-assessment incorporating a variety of self-reactions and beliefs such as feelings of self-worth and general beliefs of competence.[4] Self-esteem has been defined as a type of belief involving judgments of self-worth. It is an affective reaction indicating how a person feels about him or herself.[5] This self-assessment is quite distinct from self-efficacy perceptions, which involve cognitive judgments of personal capability.[6] So how you feel about your worth and how you feel about your performance are two different sets of perceptions and emotions. That's why we get leaders who have high levels of self-esteem yet feel inadequate to successfully meet the demands of the tasks at hand.

Self-observation (also called self-monitoring) is a performance control phase process that involves selectively attending to aspects of one's behavior or performance.[7] The more robust your self-regulating behaviors, the greater asset you'll be to your organization, church, family, etc. This ability to accurately self-assess is an important process because it helps learners differentiate between effective and ineffective performances and helps to isolate the source of error or confusion when one is performing poorly. From a social cognitive perspective, self-regulation has been defined as self-generated thoughts, feelings, and actions that are planned and cyclically adapted based on performance feedback to attain self-set goals.[8] Development of self-regulatory capabilities requires instilling a resilient sense of efficacy, as well as imparting knowledge and skills. If people are not fully convinced of their personal efficacy, "they rapidly abandon the skills they have been taught when they fail to get quick results or it requires bothersome effort". [9]

The Role of Personality in Self-Motivation

The concept of **The Big Five** personality traits is taken from psychology and includes five broad descriptive domains. It was during one of my doctoral classes, *Personality and*

Developmental Theory, that I first learned about **The Big Five**. I am no stranger to self-assessments. I have taken every strength finder and personality assessment under the sun, but I was mesmerized by this simple construct. The most popular current version of trait taxonomies suggests that there are five basic groupings, or five superordinate traits.[10] **The Big Five** personality traits form the acronym **OCEAN**.

(O) for openness to experience
(C) for conscientiousness
(E) for extraversion
(A) for agreeableness
(N) for neuroticism

These traits are used to understand the relationship between personality and various behaviors and were defined and described by various researchers during multiple periods of research. Several of these traits are used extensively in self-efficacy research and literature.

Psychologists define three aspects of individuals' personality profile, feelings, thoughts, and behaviors, that differentiate one person from the next.[11] Findings across different lines of personality research show that people who have a high sense of perceived self-efficacy in a given domain think, feel, and act differently from those who perceive themselves as inefficacious.[11] These efficacious individuals possess the self-regulation to control their inner terrain in response to their outer environment. When they encounter difficulty or failure, they ascribe failure to insufficient effort, which supports a success orientation. They quickly recover their sense of efficacy after failures or setbacks.[12] This regenerative or adaptive capacity is most closely aligned with the personality trait of extraversion (**E**).

Psychologist Joshua Coleman, co-chair of the Council on Contemporary Families, states,

> *"Psychologists now know that there is a genetic component to resilience—some kids are "dandelions" who can manage nearly any sort of strife, while others are "orchids" who wilt unless treated with the utmost care."*

Those who are high in the personality trait of **Extraversion** will exhibit an almost extra version of themselves and be much more adept at handling life's hiccups and setbacks. A regenerative nature and adaptive capacity are the two greatest keys to ensuring success in life and contentment with whatever external situations individuals encounter. Without this resiliency the individual may fold under the stresses of daily life or crash and burn in the fires of crisis.

The counter-side to this high degree of self-efficacy is expressed through ruminative inefficacious thought. Individuals with low self-efficacy depress and distress themselves and constrain and impair their level of functioning.[13] This negative, self-destructive behavior is reflected in the personality trait of neuroticism (**N**). Indeed, a growing body of evidence reveals that human accomplishments and positive well-being require an optimistic sense of personal efficacy.[14] Therefore, *"it takes a resilient sense of self-efficacy to override the numerous dissuading impediments to significant accomplishments"*.[15] Your personality has a huge amount to do with your will to succeed in life and your desire to be developed. The good news is that we can continue to refine and re-fire our intrinsic traits up until our last breath. The bad news is, we often don't want to do the work or accept the ownership that this metamorphosis entails.

Enthusiasm Makes the Difference

Many of you reading this book, personally met or listened to recordings of my father. His name was Charles "Tremendous" Jones, and he was—well—tremendous! My childhood years were a cross between boot camp and a sitcom. These formative times were intensely focused and results oriented, but also incredibly fun and spontaneous. My father wrote a book in 1967 which has never gone out of print and has been translated into 15 different languages. The title of this best-seller is *Life is Tremendous*, and the tagline is *Enthusiasm Makes a Difference*. My father was right; the main ingredient to a tremendous life is enthusiasm. Do it with passion, or don't do it at all.

Life responds in kind to our level of enthusiasm or lack thereof. The famous historian, Arnold Toynbee, said, *"Apathy can only be overcome by enthusiasm, and enthusiasm can only be aroused by two things: first, an IDEAL which takes the imagination by storm, and second, a definite intelligible PLAN for carrying that ideal into practice."*

If there's anything that catches people's attention and causes them to sit up and take notice of what you're saying or doing, it's ENTHUSIASM! The word enthusiasm is derived from two Greek words: "En", which means IN, and "theos", which means GOD. So, enthusiasm literally means "in God", or "God in us"! Thus, the truly enthusiastic person is one who acts and speaks as if he were possessed by God! There's a great management quip that goes, *"If you're not fired with enthusiasm, you'll be fired with enthusiasm!"* So, the person most responsible for lighting the proverbial fire under one's self is—YOU!

Driving Change

Change doesn't just happen and you can't manage change; you must drive and lead change. Change is simultaneously the greatest and the scariest thing that can happen to a human being. There's an old line that says change is only welcome from a vending machine. Many of us have had a love hate relationship with change most of our lives. When we need it, we refuse it; and when we are in our comfort zone, we push change out of the realm of possibility until the pain of not changing is intolerable.

I spent twelve years in the military and learned to love acronyms. I still enjoy using them in my current position. Here's a great acronym for **CHANGE** that I came up with during my research for this book: **Constantly Harnessing Anything Necessary to Grow Exponentially!** That's what change is. You've got to exchange what you are for what you want to be and that means something is not going to be as it was before. Something has to go away—the old version of you—so that the new one may emerge.

All change is death—the dying away of something that used to be a part of your life. Maybe that's why change is so hard for so many people. During my doctoral research, I read an article titled, *Change or Die*, in which people with serious heart disease were told if they did not change, their time on earth would be cut short. What are the odds of them changing? **One in nine!** That's right; even when faced with a crisis like death we fight change. If you are one of the few who love change, rejoice! But if you're like the rest of us, you're going to need some tools to get you on your way and to keep you on your way.

What Does it Really Take to Infuse Change?

Studies in neuroscience began to uncover, in progressively more complete form, the neurological origins of behavior.[16] While medical doctors are currently using brain plasticity research to deal with the effects of neurological impairment and illness in patients, the behavioral scientists and clinicians focus on the adaptive capacity to "retrain the brain". This experimentation has broad implications for behavioral transformation, or in the case of this book, unlocking potential.[17]

Not so many years ago, mainstream neuroscience and neurological medicine contended that plasticity was limited to an early childhood epoch—a "critical" or "sensitive period." Research now purports that brain remodeling can be induced on a large scale at any age of life.[18] So that means that old dogs actually can learn new tricks! The main difference in adult cognitive changes versus those during childhood is that the older brain's moment-by-moment control of change is permitted only when the specific contextual conditions that enable or trigger plasticity are met.[19] A crisis could be the context that induces a change of feelings, thinking, and behavior in an individual and often, that is when we are forced into making a change.

The triggers that positively enable plasticity include focused attention, goal seeking stimulus, arousal, unexpected or surprising events, and the attainment of a reward, all components of a crisis.[20] During the past 40 years, neuroscience has determined that the brain is continuously plastic when confronted with certain **sparks**[21], thus the ability for each of us to respond to life events and goals with creativity and resiliency is a reality.

Where Does Change Happen?

We've all heard someone describe a change of heart, but what exactly does this mean? Is this sentiment or activity different than changing your mind? Fans of Napoleon Hill can recite one of his most famous quotes, *"Whatever the mind can conceive and believe, it can achieve."* The topic of mindfulness is as massive an attraction as servant leadership. Speakers are paid big money to address this topic. So, doesn't it stand to reason that if I put my mind to something, it will produce the desired results or change?

Are mindfulness and heartfulness equally potent as catalysts, or is one more important than the other? The answer is one **is** more important than the other. Those of us who have had something crystal clear in our minds that has not panned out in our reality, have experienced this misfire firsthand. Now you can see and understand the reason why conceiving and believing by itself is not enough.

A change of heart must precede any other change and here is why. Our hearts and our minds are inextricably linked. Proverbs 23:7 says, *"for he is the kind of person who is always thinking about the cost. "Eat and drink," he says to you, but his heart is not with you."* Ezekiel 36:26 says, *"I will give you a new heart and put a new spirit in you; I will remove from you your heart of stone and give you a heart of flesh."* This renewed heart or spirit are one in the same and both represent the area where a new principle of life is placed; where new light is infused, where the new **SPARK** ignites new purposes and resolutions. A new heart must be in place before the renewed mind can begin to manifest itself.

A new heart is also the place where new affections are placed, and new desires are formed. I recently experienced this when I entered the covenant of marriage after being a perfectly happy and self-sufficient bachelorette for 23 years. Before I could wrap my head around changing my marital status, I had to have a change of heart. The heart enshrouds your motives, houses your pain, and shields your inner being. It is also the only thing capable of changing you, and hence, changing the world. First the new heart, then the new mind, then the new behaviors. A new heart equals a new nature equals a new you. So, are you ready for a change of heart? I know you are.

Change Can Only Transpire from the Inside Out

The subtitle to this book is *"Five Essentials to Ignite the Greatness Within"*. After decades of trying to find the right externals to bring out the best version of myself via the right career, the right job, the right boss, the right salary, the right friends, or the right partner, I finally realized that nothing external was going to help me find the 'me' I was truly looking for. You've heard the analogies of the caterpillar and the egg. The potential is inside and takes time and traction to move beyond present circumstances and morph into the next best version of our self.

I am appointing you the title of Chancellor of the Ministry of Interior, YOUR Interior. In Matthew 23, Jesus scolded the Pharisees, calling them greedy and blind hypocrites for placing so much importance on outward cleanliness, but having no regard for inward purity. Again, everything we produce outwardly is the result of the motives of our heart. So, first and foremost, we must make sure we have our inner house in order. There's a great phrase from the early 1900's, *Trip the Light Fantastic*, meaning that we must dance to our own music with life as our partner. To do this we have to invest everything we have now. Only high risk yields great returns, and the reason you are reading this book is to ignite the greatness within.

Not Just Another Self-Help Plan

The purpose of this book isn't to mold you, but to unfold you. Not even you know the potential lying in wait, but by the end of this book you will have the tools to ignite your internal combustion. You will understand what motivates you to become the greatest version of yourself and the tools you need to make it happen. There is an intrinsic motivation that creates the initial **SPARK**, but without the extrinsic fuel to keep the fire going, it'll eventually smother and die. This book addresses the two sides of the coin you must keep flipping back and forth.

When Joan of Arc was asked why God would need an army to accomplish his plans, she replied, *"We will do the fighting, and God will supply the victory."* In other words, you do have greatness already within you imprinted by the creator of the universe. However, you do need to complete the work required to bring this greatness front and center onto the world's stage. God and you, what an unstoppable team. Igniting greatness requires both of you coming together to "Trip the Light Fantastic." God is not going to drag you to your destiny, and he will never leave you without a partner on the dance floor of life.

Closing Remarks Before Ignition

This book will enable you to rewrite the script of your life every day, in every way. In order to guarantee success (and I guarantee success) you must be dialed into two mindsets. First, you must see value in the goal you have set before you. Your goals can't be the dreams of your family or friends; they must belong to you and you alone and be something you hold very dear. The second point is that you must have a reasonable expectation of success. There's a world of difference between a daydream, a pipe dream, and a true dream. The first is fantasy, the second fiction, and the third is fact.

Remember the iconic quote from Buzz Lightyear in Toy Story, "To infinity and beyond!" Going from earth to eternity requires the realization that your journey never ends. Everyone has been created to reach beyond their grasp. Do you believe this truth? Will you allow it to transform you? God wastes nothing, not even our darkness because the darkness is where the seeds of desire are pushed out of dormancy and into growth mode.

The first part of this book goes into the theory of motivation and the great leadership term called 'self-efficacy'. I studied it at length during my doctoral research. I am obsessed with capturing in a bottle the lightning of what makes one person get up to fight another day, while the other one turns and runs away. It's so much more than luck or circumstance; its resiliency and an adaptive capacity.

We'll look at length in regard to what the research and leadership literature say about motivation and how it comes into play between leaders, followers, co-workers, family, and friends. I want to get you grounded on the science of success; that motivation does not have to be a mystery, and that there is a step by step methodology to unlock the best version of yourself. You, and only you, must have the ambition, drive, and desire to modify your feelings, thoughts, behaviors, and habits. We can have a great tribe of cheerleaders, mentors, and benefactors, but it's up to us to put our noses to the grindstone to get to—and keep at—work.

The second part of this book will help identity your tremendous triggers. What gets me going in the morning may not work for you. Different strokes for different folks. That is the gospel truth. We are all coded and gifted in such diverse ways, yet inextricably linked in this body called humanity. There are two sides to the coin of motivation: Internal Intentionality and External Entities. If you only have one, you won't get where you want to go and you'll be on a hamster wheel going nowhere in life. I know, I've been there. If you are ready to launch out of your Habitrail and onto the Tremendous Habit Trails of life, then read on and prepare for ignition!

SPARK

ONE

SINGULARITY: RECALIBRATE
ON EXPECTATION

If you don't see it before you see it, you won't see it.

"The main thing is to keep the
main thing the main thing."

—Stephen Covey

Are you feeling exhausted—like a hamster on a wheel that keeps chasing after the next big thing because you're hearing from all the so-called experts that this is what you're supposed to be doing? Do you run here and there depending on what podcast you listen to or conference you attend? Or have you become such a jack or jane of all trades that your customer is unclear as to what it is exactly that you provide to reduce friction in their lives. Or maybe you've picked up and put down so many new ideas and projects that you're honestly not even sure which one you should be focusing on. If you are all thrust and no vector you are going to feel and be bone weary and out of gas. Even my father suffered a bout of chronic fatigue syndrome mid-career; it can happen to even the strongest of us. This first chapter is all about getting so dialed in that you can keep an intense focus and avoid those costly distractive detours.

The Most Important Ask of All

In 1 Kings 3, King Solomon had a dream where God came to him and asked him what he should give him. Solomon loved the Lord and hungered to serve him as his father King David had. Solomon also realized he had some big shoes to fill and a monumental task in leading and literally rebuilding a nation. Solomon's request is the most important key to unlocking the greatness within.

*He asked for wisdom in the form of
an understanding mind to govern and in the form
of discernment so he could sort good from evil;
all so that he might properly rule God's people.*

I learned early in running a business that praying for success was futile, for many reasons. I may not be ready for success or perhaps I may be so selfish that my idea of success wouldn't be congruent with the needs of the entity. So, I stopped praying for success and started praying for clarity. Without clarity, you can never dial in exactly where your **Resources** need to be directed. Without clarity, you never know what questions to ask and how to engage in ethical and strategic decision-making. Without clarity you cannot set boundaries. Without clarity you cannot zero in on **Singularity**.

Please take your time on this first essential because if you get it right, the other points in this book naturally unfold. The key to **Singularity** is to get so dialed into exactly what you *need* to see that you phase out everything that falls outside that tightly delineated mark. Notice how I said 'need' and not 'want'. There's a world of difference between the two and it's taken me my whole life to figure this out.

What you need to see has intrinsic value in affecting positive changes in your own and others' lives. What we want to see may be self-serving, deluded, or a false assumption. When you dial into your **Singularity**, you'll find that your wants and your needs have become 100 percent aligned. You'll have to say no in response to other options so you can focus all of your energy and **Resources** on that *one* thing. Let's dive into the difference so you can see what I am talking about.

I remember a professor in my doctoral program giving us some sage advice. Everything in our years of coursework was geared toward the completion of our final dissertation. To achieve that end each professor took the time to continue walking us toward our desired field of study. But first, we had to determine and limit our desired area of research. The metaphor the professor used was of great help. Think of a tree. Next, think of a branch. Next, think of a leaf, and then think of a cell. Then think of a molecule. And then think of an atom. That atom is your dissertation topic. That is how tightly focused you want your dissertation topic to be. <u>This is how tightly focused your goal should be.</u>

I knew I couldn't just write about leadership, although leadership is the focus of my Ph.D. What about leadership? Well, let's focus on crisis leadership. Okay, what about crisis leadership? Well, let's look at the role of followers in helping a leader deal with the crisis. What exactly about the followers do you want to research? Well, the self-efficacy of individuals and how that contributed to leader emergence in navigating an organizational crisis. Ta dah! I had my topic.

Resist the Temptation to be a Jack or Jane of all Trades

When I first returned home to run the family business, best-selling author and speaker Bruce Wilkinson was at a donor conference I attended. He asked me, "Out of the three things you spend the most time doing—writing, speaking, and operations—which one do you want to focus your energy on?" In my naiveté I told him all three! Bruce was right and I was wrong. I needed to get clear on where I wanted to drive this second-generation business. Just because my father was a world-renowned motivational speaker should I try and be one too? I had decades of operational expertise, but hadn't I come home to awaken my untapped entrepreneur and not as a project manager in a different setting? I had always dreamed of being a writer as well, but could I actually make a living writing through people purchasing my books?

According to leadership literature, you will only do one thing at a time with excellence. This was a tough point for multi-taskers like me to acknowledge and internalize. The more we start and take on the more we dilute our power. Staying on point is critical for those of us serving on boards, going back to school, raising children or pets, or running small businesses where **Resources** are at a premium. Stay in your lane of core competency.

No matter how much I equally loved each of the aspects of my business, I needed to hone in on one at a time or I was not going to get traction with any of them. Life will keep pruning you down to the stump until there is no doubt what is left and which direction you are going to grow. Trust me, it does. So, if you can do it to yourself before life does it to you, it'll be to your advantage because you'll save a whole lot of time, energy, and **Resources** (and crying towels!).

If your mind is cluttered, as most of ours are, I recommend a simple solution to get your clarity juices flowing. In your life, incorporate a 20/20/20 rule. Every day, take an hour and commit doing three things; 20 minutes of reading, meditating or praying; 20 minutes of decluttering which may include cleaning off your desk, assembling a bag of unused clothing for donation, or even writing a long-overdue letter; 20 minutes of activity which could be jogging, stretching, yoga, running, anything to get the blood and oxygen flowing to your head. This exercise is a brilliant way to get you moving and focused.

Inch by inch, life's a cinch.
Yard by yard, life is hard.

No Blessings for a Divided Soul

There are two groups of people; ones who have a hard time getting started and ones who have a hard time getting focused. We'll talk about the first group more under the **Resources** chapter later in this book. The second group I mentioned eats and breathes activity. If we do not have a million things on our plates, we get forlorn and depressed. For these people (of which I am one) **Singularity** isn't about what you are going to do (there's never a shortage of that) but rather what are you going to focus on. There's an old saying that there are no blessings for a divided soul. You can be focused on two godly options and still have issues. One of Satan's favorite tools is to keep you so busy that you lose focus and experience mission drift. We need to be hyper-vigilant concerning which moving pieces we are going to direct our energy toward. Direction is so much more important than speed. Many are going nowhere fast.

Another key element of **Singularity** is to write down your goal. There is something about writing it down that primes the ignition switch. My father used to say, *"Every time we write down and talk about a goal, we push the button to start the success mechanism."* My rescue dogs taught me that if you chase two rabbits, they both get away. They were right. Stay focused and don't get distracted.

Clarity Blockers

We tend to focus on recognizing talent and cultivating capability and place a lot less emphasis on what is hindering our character development. The risk in doing this is missing things in our life that need pruning. Are you receptive to revelation? Even though we all dream dreams, your dream can't just be rooted in positive thinking but needs to be grounded in reality thinking. Your reality must also be rooted in truth; truth that is based on principles and not on our personalities; dreams that are based on character and not charisma.

Lastly, know that **Singularity** will involve a stepping away from *Mount Majority*. You are going to march to the beat of your own drum. John Wanamaker said, *"To every man there must come a day when he must separate and act alone."* Don't expect a cheering section either. This is your path to walk, and if you walk it alone so be it. I have seen so many people step out to follow their dream only to fold at the lack of applause. They let the deafening silence defeat them. If this happens, you know it was never really about the purpose, but rather all about the person, not the experience, but rather the ego. If our **Singularity** is not greater than ourselves, we'll drop the vision thing like a hot potato.

Clarity Amplifiers

For me, the *what* has always been more important than the *why*. The answer to my why question is clear; to help others live their most tremendous life because of the many people who had poured knowledge into me over the years. Before we get started in creating our life, there are central decisions we must make for ourselves. My father, Charlie "Tremendous" Jones, referred to them in the Life-Changing Classic, *The Three Decisions*. Once you plant your flag, you are free to develop your execution strategy. If you have not nailed down these three decisions, you'll waffle and experience a repeated lack of traction and life of frustration. Often, the source of this failure of clarity is too much noise.

You can't hear what you're supposed to do with your life if you aren't in an environment conducive to listening. There is a ridiculous amount of noise and clutter flooding our modern-day minds. Here are some simple things to eliminate any spiritual, physical, or mental blockage preventing the blessing pipeline from being opened fully.

The first imperative key is to take one day a week and Sabbath. According to Dr. Henry Cloud, *"Monday blues may be about how depleted we are from the lack of intimacy in our lives. We can't be refinishers with an empty relational tank."*[1]

Sabbathing isn't a thing of the past when life wasn't so frenetic and disconnected. We need it more now than at any other time in the history of mankind. Silence is an essential requirement for today, more so now than ever since we have such a hard time silencing all the noise that is infecting our brains. This time of rest and solitude allows you to hear what direction you should be going.

Where and *why* you need to go is already in you.
The key is unlocking it with the activation of the *what*.

Although we love to talk to others and listen to podcasts, we must make sure we take the time to recharge without further draining our energy stores so we can hear what's to come next.

The second critical step to gaining clarity is to cut the cord. One of my favorite bands, Ned's Atomic Dustbin, has a song titled, *Kill Your Television.* You say, "Ms. Tracey, how will I ever know what is going on in the world?" Well, I'll tell you one thing television is not good for... finding out the truth. There are plenty of blogs, websites, and peer-reviewed journals you can subscribe to in order to stay current on what's important to your future plans and that requires your action. You can watch whatever show you deem healthy enough to enter your brain through a streaming service. Don't allow any of that other garbage to infect your space. Turn it off now.

Third, here is my number one activity for gaining clarity: Assemble your closest group of critically thinking supporters and speak freely to bounce ideas. Have them present worst-case scenarios so you can contingency plan. Consider any and all options, even writing out a pro and con sheet. Draw two circles, one with all the items that show where you are now (real) and the second a circle with all the items that show where you would like to be (ideal). Now you can see in front of you what needs to be left behind and what you need to bring forward. Other clarity gainers include books, online tests, mentors, prayer, journaling, networking events, mission trips, ministry, and volunteerism. Many people have found exactly what they were looking for by just being open to participating in service to others.

Peaks and Valleys are Part of Singularity

As you ascend the mountain of life, it's imperative you jettison the baggage that is no longer needed (which can include certain people and programs) so you can suit up for the next leg of the journey. This act isn't mean-spirited or harmful; it's life. (If you struggle with this part, read *Boundaries* by Dr. Cloud and Dr. Townsend.) We suit up differently in our daily lives depending on the time of year, and the same is true for seasons of life. The key to **Singularity** is to shift, not drift. You'll change lanes in life and that's okay. Just make sure all roads are still leading as directly as possible to your final destination.

The bottom line is this; the truth is in you. It's just a matter of dialing it in so you can see it clearly. This first step, **Singularity**, will take time and you may have some false starts where you begin in one direction only to realize you need to change course. That is completely acceptable. I have never been one of those people who instinctively or intuitively knew exactly what I wanted to do with my life. It took me seven years and four schools to get my bachelor's degree. If you happen to be one of these folks who are gifted with clarity at a young age, you can move more quickly through this initial stage.

For the rest of us, it is crucial to take time to really land on our **Singularity**. This is the bedrock foundation on which you are going to build your life house. Make sure you have a good, long, honest talk with yourself to understand what it is that you're driving toward. Many people get hung up on the *"why"*. Personally, I have never been too focused on this question. If I know *what* it is, the *why* becomes negligible. Right now, you need to focus on WHAT; WHY is overrated; don't be a "why"ner. If you aren't getting clarity, then do something, anything, because motion tends to uncover different landscapes and previously unrecognized assumptions or faulty thinking.

Clarity is Independent of Circumstances

If you're stuck on the *why*, you need to get counsel because you haven't taken your eyes off yourself You are fixated on your individuality and until you "die to self" you will never unlock your innate personality. *Why* is driven by insecurity. One of the most impactful books I have read in my life is Viktor Frankl's classic, *Man's Search for Meaning*. Frankl was a celebrated Austrian psychiatrist and Holocaust survivor who discovered the single most important factor that allowed men to survive was teaching them to hold onto a future goal. My favorite quote from this life changing book is, *"Ultimately, man should not ask what the meaning of his life is, but rather must recognize that it is he who is asked. In a word, each man is questioned by life; and he can only answer to life by answering for his own life; to life he can only respond by being responsible."*

Ask yourself *why* as a routine diagnostic, not as a directive. You can remind yourself *why* you are doing something when you need an extra boost of motivation (and you will). When you gain clarity, you'll know what conversations to have. You'll also know what opportunities to say no to in order to preserve your **Resources** and reputation

In the perennial best-seller, *Think and Grow Rich*, author Napoleon Hill says the most important factor in success is something he calls "definiteness of purpose". Definiteness of purpose is defined as having a goal to arrive at and working toward that goal. After interviewing 500 millionaires and distilling the common threads they all attributed to an individual's success, definiteness of purpose ranked number one. That is why **Singularity** is needed first and foremost before you can unlock the greatness within.

Your Legacy Is Your Record of Service

Even though books and motivation were a constant in my life since my birth, I had to get clear on whether running the "family business" was what I was put on earth to do. In 2008, not only was my father fading, but the organization's founder was as well. In those last three months as my father succumbed to the effects of cancer, I made the trek from Saint Louis, MO to Harrisburg, PA as often as I could.

During those visits, my father never asked me to come home and run the business. We had touched briefly on this option throughout the years, usually when I was transitioning from one career to the next—which I did often. I did find out many years later he told many others his goal was to have me come back to run the business. As his time on earth was ending, I became more agitated that he didn't ask me to come back and pick up the mantel of leadership. Did he think I couldn't handle it? Was he convinced that I would be bored or over-whelmed? It was two days before he graduated to be with the Lord, that I made the decision I was going to transition out of my previous work and come home to run the business. When I shared this with my father in one of our last earthly conversations, he smiled, squeezed my hand and whispered that I would take the business places he never could. That was the extent of our succession planning. I knew with complete certainty that I needed to come back to run the business. My singular focus was keeping the core, but growing and evolving new variations of the tremendous traits that DNA brings.

As I reflected on what transpired, I realized my father knew I needed to figure out what I wanted. I suspect he also knew that decision would take years. He understood that what he wanted me to do needed to have the blessing of my intentionality and God's timing. He watched me go from professional field to professional field; living all over the world and growing my experience bag. The one thing I had never done, however, was really think about what Tracey C. Jones wanted to do next with her life in terms of what was best for me. Every professional move I ever made was based on opportunity, title, salary, location, or the chance to go on a new adventure. Although I had never been an entrepreneur, I got clarity very quickly, realizing that now was the time to take the leap. Some opportunities only come once in life, and this was one of them.

Out of the mess, comes the message.
Out of the test, comes the testimony.

There were two things that gave me clarity to make this call. The first was a spiritual presence in the corner of the room I sensed several days before my father passed. The presence was also above my father pulling back a curtain as his soul departed his body. This was not a physical presence, but rather an angelic one that was more felt than seen. The angel gave me an overwhelming sense of knowing. Receiving angelic guidance is one of the best ways you can be sure you are in line with your life's purpose. Remember, angels are divine messengers. One major sign that you're in the presence of angels is a sense of universal knowing. Have you ever had a big decision to make and then seemingly out of nowhere, you know exactly what to do next? I must admit I was a bit embarrassed to mention what had happened to anyone for years. But that was because of my lack of spiritual maturity and understanding. Now I know how important it is to share with others how the Holy Spirit can help us with our **Singularity**.

One day I told my mother what I had experienced and she looked at me and said, "You too?" Had I not had that angelic visit; I probably would have stayed on my current professional path of defense contracting in Washington, DC for years to come. Coming home to be an entrepreneur was just so far outside my realm of previous experience that if the spirit of God had not singularly positioned me to know what I was to do, I'm not sure I would have figured it out on my own. So, make sure you stay open to all types of signs as you search for your **Singularity**. Clarity can come in all types of inspiration. If you want a remarkable book on hearing God's word and how it is a living and active presence in your life, read *Talking with God* by French theologian François Fénelon.

SIB-KIS

In my father's book, *Life is Tremendous*, he outlined the SIB-KIS principle: ***See it Big; Keep it Simple.*** He would also often quote Stephen Covey, *"The main thing is to keep the main thing the main thing."* As you can see from reading his book, he was so successful and impactful because he was so focused. As you get traction on your goals, you will immediately be presented with numerous other possibilities. This is the direct result of you taking action which opens up the realm of previously unrecognized or unattainable possibilities. My father used to also say, *"Nothing works...until you work it!"* Now is the time to stay focused on what you are doing. As Jim Collins said, *"Good is the enemy of great"*. So, while you may be good at multiple things you can only truly be the greatest at one thing.

I spent my years in the Air Force as an aircraft maintenance officer on fighter jets—F-15s and F-16s. Pilots must have their flight plans filed before they leave the ground for many obvious reasons; they might run out of fuel or end up in enemy territory or a no-fly zone. The same is true for us. Before we launch out into the wild blue yonder, we need to know the destination. We need to set our expectations. You may be asking

'Why? What's wrong with just winging it?' Wrong expectations lead to great disappointments, wasted precious **Resources**, and lost opportunities. Life is too short to have this happen.

When you fail to plan, you plan to fail.

This inescapable truth takes aging, seasoning, maturing, and learning to live. I can still hear my father telling others you're wet behind the ears until you're 55. He was right again! Gaining **Singularity** is a lifelong journey that grows as we do. It's never as easy as just "figuring it out". Rather, life has a way of heightening our awareness with every experience we gain. Speaking of awareness, self-awareness is listed as one of the five top traits of emotional intelligence (EQ). Not awareness of others, but awareness of self. Too many times we focus on teaching others what they need to go after in life, but we fail to take the time to get ourselves accurately oriented.

Your points of reference will shift as will your desires and surroundings. Don't be alarmed when they do. This is life's way of letting you know it's time for a transition. The book of Ecclesiastes has one overarching theme, to everything there is a season—prosperity, calamity, life, death, sickness, and health. There will be things and people that come into your life for a season and then depart. Your **Singularity** is tied only to your internal compass, and not to external people, places, and things. I say this because in life you may lose a job, a relationship, an opportunity, a deal, or promotion, where you think you've missed the boat forever. Take heart, friend; you are simply about to begin the next leg of your journey. But, make sure you realign your site and file a new flight plan for life.

An Integrated Life is a Tremendous Life

The root word of Integer is "one". An integral life is one that is congruent in all aspects. A friend recently shared a three-part question his company asks all new hires.

First, how would you describe yourself?
Second, how would your friends and coworkers describe you?
Third, how would your boss or leaders describe you?

The answers need to be as congruent as possible; otherwise you're dealing with an unformed or malformed or squishy character.

For example, you may have your financial house in order but your health may be horrible due to some bad habits you will not break. You may maintain a strict code of business ethics but do not honor your personal vows to your family. You may be responsible for making thousands of command decisions each day, yet not be able to discipline your own children living under your roof. You need to maintain discipline, boundaries, and focus in all areas of your life. You'll never be as effective as you can be until you fumigate your entire life and surround yourself with other top dogs who hate fleas as much as you do.

I learned a great deal about whole life integration as a young girl. I grew up watching family, work, spirituality, and fun all rolled into one tremendous blend. My father would travel across the country speaking and selling books and he would load all six of us kids, my mother, luggage, and cases of books into various sizes of RVs and off we'd go! One of our favorite family memories is from a trip we took from Camp Hill, Pennsylvania to Mexico City, Mexico in a Volkswagen bus with a pop-up top. I was five years old at the time, but still have memories of rolling over in my sleeping bag onto a cactus, hearing my mother scream when she saw I was drinking the water, and crying at the bullfight when the bull got stuck with the javelins. These adventures played out time and time again as the Jones pack trekked thousands of miles and met thousands of people.

Everything in life we experienced had an element of merriment but was also purposeful. I learned early on how to live a harmonious life whereby I was not separating individual segments of myself from others. When people ask me if I ever take a vacation, I think, "Now why would I do that? Isn't all of life one big vacation?" When you live life as a whole person you can be the same person in each of the rooms of your life. An added benefit to **Singularity** is that it equips you with stability so no matter what the circumstances, you can fire on all cylinders. First Corinthians 10:31 says, *"So whether you eat or drink or whatever you do, do it all for the glory of God."*

Singularity is Vision

In my father's book, *The Price of Leadership*, he lists *Vision* as one of the wages you'll have to pay in order to lead. Vision isn't something mystical that only the super smart or gifted can see. Vision is simply being able to see things as they are. He goes on to say, *"We cannot pay the price of leadership without knowing where we are going and what we are doing."* Think back to the example of Solomon from the beginning of this chapter. He understood this concept. He knew how difficult leadership is so he asked for the wisdom to see what needed to be done.

Singularity is synonymous with vision and as the scriptures say where there is no vision, the people perish.[2] When you know the *what*, you know which questions to ask and the conversations you need to have. This helps clear off the non-essentials that steal your time and **Resources** away. Vision in the form of **Singularity** gives an intense focus enabling you to drive towards valued added meetings, conversations, partnerships, and habits. Anything that doesn't make the cut gets left by the side of the road.

Value Congruence

Your **Singularity** is also going to reflect your values. So, once you've got clarity, you'll need to look for leaders and organizations whose values you share so you can be professionally yoked. Otherwise, there's going to be a painful divergence in the future. The term leader-follower value congruence is defined as the perceived similarity in values held by a leader and a follower.[3] Research suggests that personal values facilitate understanding of the relationship between leaders and followers.[4]

Do not join an organization that is misaligned with the values and convictions you hold dear. If you do, it will just be a matter of time before the implosion and you will lose—after all, it is not your entity. You'll also kill your **Singularity** in the process because how can you be focused on something that you do not agree with or hold dear in your heart? It's not fair to you, and it's not fair to the organization. I jumped at many opportunities because of the increase in salary, prestigious title, or ability to live across the globe. Although I worked hard, it was obvious I was speaking a different value language than the organization. In the end, I knew I had to go. Wait for the value fit. You'll be thankful in the end you did.

Can My Singularity Change?

In *The Three Decisions*, my father outlines the only decisions in life we will ever have to make:

Who you're going to live your life with.
What are you going to live your life doing.
Who are you going to live your life for.

Some people get these decisions dialed in early in their lives while others of us have suffered the pain of losing a life partner or life's work. There will always be a shifting pattern of relationships and opportunities. You may get a Mission Complete calling before you were expecting one. You will also see that intimate friendships change at each level and only the collaborations of the highest and most pure order remain with you throughout your life. That is okay; don't stress out about these changes. Worry only if they are not happening. The price of growth is transformation, in every area of your life.

So, the answer is yes, your **Singularity** can change. As mentioned earlier, the book of Ecclesiastes makes it clear that to everything there is a season; sometimes brought on by mistakes we make, other times through no fault of our own. The rain falls on the just and the unjust so get used to it. We do fall out of love as we go through vision changes in life. We get older and more seasoned. What may have seemed like our life's dream may change as we develop a heightened sense of capability and discernment.

Never be afraid to adapt your **Singularity** as you go through life. As we transform our **Singularity** should shift, not drift. You are going to change. So does our internal viewing mechanism. What once suited us, is no longer a good fit; maybe we've grown out of it or maybe we can declare Mission Complete and prepare for our next set of orders. Remember, as your character develops throughout your life, so will your levels of revelation and degrees of restoration. In other words, we get smarter, more sensitive, more discerning. We get thicker skins and softer hearts, shedding our thin skins and hard hearts.

Kick Fear to the Curb

One of my top five books is a little paperback called, *Hung by the Tongue,* by Francis P. Martin. Our clients order this book by the thousands, so I knew I needed to read this gem. One of the greatest points in this book is that faith activates God and fear activates Satan. You will always live to the level of your faith or fear. If you are still struggling with your **Singularity,** I have a 100 percent guaranteed solution—do something for someone else. When you focus on ministry to others your definiteness of purpose immediately becomes linked to an eternal purpose. This is the highest order of calling and one any leader will tell you they eventually arrive at after years of ascending and descending other peaks and valleys. There is no guaranteed job, promotion, partner, spouse, health, house, car, or raise. Each of these things can be whisked away at a moment's notice. Oswald Chambers said, *"It is not that God makes us beautifully rounded grapes, but that he squeezes the sweetness out of us."* Focus on yourself to see how you can be used in as many ways as possible. This sense of self-expenditure is a surefire way to ignite your **Singularity** sensors.

The more we serve, the more intentional we become.

Your **Singularity** must be tied to one thing and one thing only; that which cannot be destroyed by time, inflation, or atrophy. Whatever you lean on for your purpose, make sure it lasts. Your **Singularity** must last an eternity. I realized this in my mid-40's. I had wonderful careers with amazing people living all over the world. But in the end, I found myself asking what any of it mattered in the grand scheme of things. My life was all about transacting time for money, and I found myself realizing I needed so much more. My motivation could no longer be satisfied by a meal ticket in the form of a salary or in the form of power which came through a promotion. There had to be more to my work than these things.

Mark 11:24 says, *"Therefore I tell you, whatever you ask for in prayer, believe that you have received it, and it will be yours."* **Singularity** takes a lot of time in prayer. We need hear what God is telling us to do next. We must listen to know if he is in the mix of what we want to do and where we want to go. Edwin Louis Cole said, *"God will finish what he authors, but he is not obligated to finish what he has not authored."* Not just any **Singularity** will do. It needs to be God's **Singularity**. Therefore, make sure you know your marching orders are truly from above before you go into battle. After that, it's one battle plan at a time; one step at a time.

Final Thoughts

In James 2:14 it states that *faith without works is dead* but I would also say that *works without faith is dead* as well. That's why we need to focus on the criticality of **Singularity** before digging into the importance of **Persistence**. It has been said, *"The two most important days in your life are the day you are born and the day you find out why."* You are closer to achieving that second goal than you were before you started this book. Congratulations!

Life is going to test you to see just how committed you are to your vision. I watch many people revel in the courage it took them to declare their direction, only to fold up in failure the minute someone criticized or judged them.

True courage doesn't rely on anyone else's approval.
Being the authentic you, is independent of anyone else.

We've wrongly assumed that courage equates to public adoration and acceptance. That's hog wash. Your focus is yours. We'll cover who you need to be your encouragers and help you execute your goals in chapters three and four. But for now, you're going to have to put your nose to the proverbial grindstone and get to work......and never stop.

Talk is cheap. When I was in the military, operational plans were only operational when we executed them. Vision boards are just clippings and post it notes unless you attach specific activities. Take a moment and read an excerpt from Oswald Chambers' *My Utmost for His Highest* devotional titled Vision and Reality (July 6):

We always have visions before a thing is made real.
When we realize that although the vision is real, it is
not real in us, then is the time that Satan comes in
with his temptations, and we are apt to say it is no
use to go on. Instead of the vision becoming real,
there has come the valley of humiliation.

Onto **Persistence!**

SPARK

TWO

PERSISTENCE: RECALIBRATE
OUR EFFORT

God can't work until you do.

"By perseverance the snail reached the ark."

—Charles Spurgeon

Are you feeling defeated—like no matter how hard you try you just can't seem to get any traction? Do you feel more and more like you should quit and have forgotten why you even started in the first place? Do you lay awake at night wondering, "Should I stay or should I go?" Are your habits turning out to be superficial promises lacking any real grounding when the going gets tough? Real behavior change flows out of identity change. This chapter is all about dialing in your vision so fiercely that no matter how much or how many times you want to quit....<u>you never will</u>.

For those of you who thought that 'P' was going to stand for passion keep in mind, I am much more a pragmatist than an idealist. Joseph Joubert said, *"Genius begins great works; labor alone finishes them."* The single most important factor to my success thus far in life has been my **Persistence**. I learned early in life that the quickest way to success is to cram 50 years of failure into 15. That means when the going gets tough, the tough get going! Vitamin P courses through my veins. In fact, I'm thinking of changing my name from Tremendous Tracey to Tenacious T!

All jokes aside, I get the whole passion thing. I love passion! I once got written up in an appraisal because I had too much passion! But here's the thing; passion results in impulse, but **Persistence** results in intentionality and if left unchecked, passion can morph into obsession. Let me explain; if I am passionate about something, I am on fire. I will fall on my sword for it. Passion is immediate and could have a lack of control. In the military we referred to this as all thrust and no vector. In the criminal justice system, they refer to the term *crimes of passion.*

I did my doctoral research on a crisis merger of two entities including one individual who was so absolutely convinced he was right in his actions, that he went to great lengths to stop the unification. The problem was, despite his crusade to do the right thing (in his mind), few others saw it or felt the same way. He cost folks a great deal of money and caused a lot of stress all because he was passionately convinced that he was right and they were wrong.

If you are persistent, you will stay focused on the goal regardless of anything else going on around you—whether it be a micromanager or macromanager boss, a corrupt co-worker, or a personal trial going on in your life. **Persistence** isn't about emotion, it's about habits. It's as simple—and as hard—as that. F.M. Alexander wrote, *"People do not decide their futures, they decide their habits and their habits decide their futures."*

Work is hard; it's also glorious and life giving. God worked for six days before he rested. There is a whole theology of work. Even after the fall we were given tasks to do; to have dominion over the earth and to reproduce. Nowhere does the Bible honor laziness or shun work. Check out how many times the book of Proverbs uses the word "sluggard". Nowhere is laziness to be tolerated or condoned. Laziness is the antithesis of greatness. You cannot ignite the greatness within and be lazy at the same time.

Let's tie back to our first chapter on **Singularity**. Diligence and discipline alone won't ignite the greatness within. Not all work is created equal. I have a friend who shared a great acronym for BUSY: Burdening Under Satan's Yoke. If you work your fingers to the bone, all you get is boney fingers. Paul states in 1 Corinthians 15:10 that we are to work as hard as we can and let the grace of God do the rest. There is a pronounced difference between activity and accomplishment. Not every activity is urgent or even necessary to move you forward. In fact, so much of what we do is unnecessary in the grand scheme of things. I wore a t-shirt in my younger days that read, "Look busy, Jesus is coming". It's funny, but it's also convicting. So now that you know where you're going (**Singularity**), it's time to stop dreaming and time to start scheming!

The Conversion Principle

Before you can begin working a plan, the plan must first be workable. Everything this side of Heaven is not the way it was supposed to be. God created a magnificent world for us, however, there are many aspects of this world that he did not directly create. Our world worships self and is marred by the effects of sin. You do not need to teach a child to be willful or defiant. We are all born with a fallen human nature and the effects are seen and felt in every moment of our lives. Therefore, it's imperative that we operate with a sense of optimistic pragmatism; that it's going to be hard, and things aren't always going to be fair, and there will be many days when we will wonder 'What's the point?'.

Negativity is as natural as the air we breathe, but so is unleashing the conquering, victorious God seed inside every one of us. God's law is love, but we are unable to do the right thing because we are morally weak and covetous. That is why socialism will never succeed this side of Heaven. Sure, Jesus was the ultimate socialist, but none of us are righteous enough to begin to even pull off this type of ultimate holiness due to the singular fact that we are not sinless. Whenever I hear someone say that they will gladly give up what they have to help others I ask what's stopping them. If you are waiting for the government to direct your giving, I can be 100 percent sure you are not sharing what you have with anyone. Pride, greed, and lust are an ever-present part of our personalities and purposes.

We must however, never forget that the victory has already been won. This should give even the most battle-weary soldier the fortitude to carry on. The battle to persist pursuing our God directed futures is possible because of the indwelling of the Holy Spirit, the Imago Dei. Remember, when we persist, we don't do it of our own accord. That can lead to despair, burnout, and exhaustion. But when we do it infused by the Spirit—when we become Spirit walkers—that's when we can persist despite all obstacles.

Even though the battle is won, it still takes a monumental effort to live a life of excellence. Currently I work as the president of Tremendous Leadership, the business my father founded to promote his love of books. In one of our best-selling Life-Changing Classics, *The New Common Denominator of Success*, author Albert E.N. Gray writes that the only difference between a failure and a success is that the success has made a habit out of doing things the failure doesn't want to do. Talk to any successful person and they will share with you the grit and sheer determination they habitually put forth every single day in order to live life to the max.

The Big Five

As I mentioned in my introduction, I came across an incredible personality trait profile in my doctoral studies referred to as *The Big Five or OCEAN*. These are the five personality traits found in all of us. Personality psychologists define three aspects to an individuals' profiles—feelings, thoughts, and behaviors—that tend to differentiate one social actor from the next.[1] The key is to enhance or augment the first four traits (O, C, E, A) and diminish or eliminate the final one (N). Neuroticism is the destructive self-talk—stinkin' thinkin' as my father called it—that seems to always find a way into our minds. I refer to highly negative people who seem to do nothing but complain and stress out as High "N" individuals (it sounds better than telling them they have a crappy attitude). Neuroticism, or negativity, is everywhere—the news, social media, blogs, anytime you sit quietly and listen in on someone else's conversation I'll bet you ten dollars they are complaining about someone or something. It's pervasive! And it's the most natural thing for humans to engage in: verbal vomit.

This tendency found in all of us needs to be addressed because **Persistence** is all about developing positive habits to replace the negative ones. As Bing Crosby crooned, *"You've got to latch onto the positive. Eliminate the negative. Latch on to the affirmative. Don't mess with Mister In-Between."*

No more *coulda, woulda, shoulda*;
only *I can, I will, I did*!

Everything in this terrestrial realm is in a state of devolution. Look at the Second Law of Thermodynamics. It takes work to cease the disarray that is our natural state. Edwin Louis Cole said it beautifully, *"Now, everything in life must be converted from negative to positive. Even the ground must be converted by being cultivated, planted, and watered. Left to itself, in its negative state, it will only grow wild with weeds."* Remember, you can't just turn over, vacuum out, or dump the negative. You must replace the negative with the positive because your mind is a vacuum and something must replace what's been extracted.

"More is to be gained by stickability than by chasing better deals." Charlie "Tremendous" Jones

Is Quitting an Option?

Walt Disney said, *"The difference between winning and losing is most often not quitting."* Perseverance is continuing when you don't want to. Let's go back to the Big Five. C stands for Conscientiousness. Those of you who are high "C" are vigilant, focused on the task at hand, tenacious and freely accept responsibility, even for problems created by your predecessor. You are duty bound and follow through. When you make a commitment, you make it yours and you die by it. There is no Plan B when you are still working Plan A. I can remember my father telling me, *"Tracey, you can want to quit, just don't do it."* It's completely natural to want to quit. We are human and we are going to experience highs and lows. Our dreams can turn into nightmares in a split second.

Persistence is what gets you up in the morning after you said you were quitting the day before. **Persistence** is what drives you to the gym before you even think how tired you are, and boom, there you are on the treadmill. Bum Phillips, Former NFL head coach of the Houston Oilers has one of my favorite quotes of all time, *"The only discipline that lasts is self-discipline."* I get calls from people all over the world telling me they wish they could make themselves do something and I ask them, "Well, why can't you?" I know the answer. They lack self-discipline. If I was there checking in on them or calling them daily, they might do it which would be a great start. However, real discipline comes from within. When we rationalize, we tell ourselves rational lies.

> *True discipline begins when we stop making*
> *excuses and start making changes.*

Since I begin each day reading Oswald Chambers' daily devotional, *My Utmost for His Highest*, here is another one of my favorites. The September 6th metaphor of a river speaks beautifully to the topic of **Persistence**.

A river is victoriously persistent, overcoming all barriers. For a while it goes steadily on its course, but then comes to an obstacle. And for a while it is blocked, yet it soon makes a pathway around the obstacle. Or a river will drop out of sight for miles, only later to emerge again even broader and greater than ever. Do you see God using the lives of others, but an obstacle has come into your life and you do not seem to be of any use to God? Then keep paying attention to the Source, and God will either take you around the obstacle or remove it. The river of the Spirit of God overcomes all obstacles. Never focus your eyes on the obstacle or the difficulty. The obstacle will be a matter of total indifference to the river that will flow steadily through you if you will simply remember to stay focused on the Source. Never allow anything to come between you and Jesus Christ—not emotion nor experience—nothing must keep you from the one great sovereign Source.

Here's a personal example. I lost fifty pounds in 2018 (Don't worry, it was only the non-tremendous part of me!). I had heard all the justifications about middle age spread, post menopause, it just is what it is, and yet I looked around and saw women and men my age that were healthy and height-weight proportionate. If they could do it, why couldn't I? I made the commitment to sign up with my health coach and I worked the plan. I stuck with it and didn't even cheat with a piece of cake on my birthday. Now, years later, I am still working it. Even though I met and sustained my goal I still don't go back and even dabble in the habits that led me on the path of being literally large and in charge. At this point I want to be healthy and in charge. My point is that I had been on a gazillion healthy habits programs before and none of them worked. Why did this one? This one worked because I consistently worked it! More importantly, you've got to give it time and create and imbed habits. Research has shown it takes 40 days for a behavior to become a habit. Most people stay on a roll for one week and then fizzle out, wondering why the modification didn't stick. The beauty of discipline is that the more you do it, the easier it becomes.

Adversity, the Greatest Teacher of All

All of us have a past. There are things that happened earlier in life, either things done to us which produced shame, or things done by us which produced guilt. These tumultuous transitions or traumas teach us resiliency and adaptability. Everything in evolution is about growing a bigger brain. It's not the strongest who survive, but the most adaptable. Plus, we are to count it all joy when we fall into various trials and tribulations.[2] Adversity teaches us steadfastness, which gets us over life's hurdles and bumps.

Let's go back to the Big Five personality traits again, this time focusing on "E", or Extraversion. This trait is my favorite. My father was the living breathing embodiment of a high "E" individual and it was the greatest trait of all the great traits he modeled for me and so many others. Extraversion is that sense of optimism and energy that you bring to everything in your life. I like to think of it as an "extra" version of ourselves. My father used to tell me that atmosphere does not just come out of thin air; somebody must create it. Individuals that possess high degrees of Extraversion can turn up the cultural temperature and excitement in any organization they enter. I recently completed my dissertation where I studied the merger of two financial institutions that turned into a crisis event. Some of the participants interviewed saw this as one of the worst things they had ever experienced, sharing how scared and worried they were. Others barely registered any distress and looked to emerging successfully no matter how things transpired. Their comments revealed something much more than a "can do" spirit.

At least half of them shared something traumatic that had happened earlier in their lives. For one it was a sister born with severe birth defects. For others it was a mother with mental illness, a husband who had an affair, or a twin who was killed in a car accident. One individual said it best, *"When you've been through life's worst trauma and survived, everything else that happens is just bumps in the road."* Again, it's not the strongest who survive, but the most adaptable. Those who had the most difficult time with the merger were the ones who had never experienced any type of change or hardship in their earlier lives.

My father used to say, *"Things don't go wrong and break your heart so you can become bitter and give up. They happen to break you down and build you up so you can be all that you were intended to be."* The other thing adversity does is make you incredibly empathic. You can be a tremendous source of hope for others by serving as a guide or encourager. You've been to hell and lived to fight another day; so will they. Another funny thing about my father, he had been through some tough things growing up—some really tough things; extreme poverty, a broken home, abuse, and flunking out of the 8th grade.

He also went through some tough things as an adult. He had been betrayed, taken advantage of, hustled and used, and had truly been heartbroken many times in his professional career. But you never would have known it. He took each instance of brokenness as a chance to receive grace as well as to give grace. As a committed Christian, he also knew suffering was par for the course. James 1:2 tells us to count it all joy when we fall into various trials. Every time I would go to him for sympathy or a shoulder to cry on, he'd exclaim, *"Tracey, is this anything worse than what Jesus suffered?"* That ended my thumb-sucking pity party really quick! When you hit the proverbial wall, rejoice because you're about to find the way you've been searching for. As Albert Einstein so eloquently stated, *"Order is for idiots, genius can handle chaos"* and you, my friend, are a genius.

The Thorn Remains

For you readers who have seasoning under your belt, I need to address a particular thing—there will be a person, habit, experience, something—you still carry with you despite all your best efforts to dispel it and pleadings with God. These are known as our "thorns". The Apostle Paul sure had one. In fact, he pleaded with God to remove it from his side in 2 Corinthians 12:7-9. Some theologians think this torn was a physical illness; others think the thorn was a messenger sent to torment Paul and defeat his spirit and to stop him from ministry.

Paul actually refers to the thorn as a messenger of Satan sent to vex him lest he grow exalted in his flesh. The apparent purpose of this thorn was beneficial. Its intent was to keep Paul from conceit on account of his visions and revelations which otherwise might have given him a reason to boast. I watch many speakers or authors get defeated when someone takes shots at them, spreads falsehoods, or creates discord for them. There is a real potential for this as you seek to move forward. When you encounter these messengers of Satan always remember, thorns are there to keep pride at bay. You won't persist past these thorns so don't try to. You will however, stay grounded as a result of them; and the truest position of pure **Persistence** is found on our knees.

Character is Better than Charisma

Now, let me give you a word of advice that will save you heartache and prevent you from quitting or redirecting. It inevitably happens that when you're dialed into your direction and focused in on your target, suddenly your eyes wander to see what everyone else is doing. Guess what? It appears that everyone else is doing so much better than you! You begin to doubt yourself. You wonder if your efforts are worth it. There must be something I'm doing wrong because everyone else is reaping the benefits and I got nada! This is where character kicks in. Charisma is a flash in the pan and most of us are old enough to know that things are never quite as they appear. Teddy Roosevelt has a great quote, *"Comparison is the thief of joy."* He's right. You should be so focused on your own goals, that you scarcely have time to check out what everyone else is doing. Who cares what they are doing anyway? You do "you" and let them do "them".

Remember Bruce Wilkinson's comments to me back in Chapter One? He said something to me during that same encounter that gave me the dogged determination I needed to never give up. Here I am, this newbie small minnow in a sea of huge best-selling authors and million-dollar speakers! How could this Air Force Veteran, hybrid engineer, analytic, possibly compete? Bruce asked me if I turned a profit that year and I told him yes, albeit a modest one. He then told me I was more successful than many of the other speakers and writers out there who may be drawing in bigger streams of revenue, but who also had greater costs which surpassed their revenue! In other words, no profit!

That was such an encouragement to me. I knew I may not be on the cover of Success Magazine or the New York Times Best Seller list (not that I don't have aspirations), but I was running a successful, profitable small business which, by the way, is the backbone of the US economy. Suddenly my feelings of inadequacy left. I had operational gifting and I was going to play to that strength as I explored other opportunities in my field. What a blessing it was to never have any debt in this business and to have the capital to invest back into it. The other thing I had to fully wrap my head and heart around was that I was not responsible for the financial outcome, God was.

Remember the angelic presence I sensed in Chapter One? That's how I knew I was exactly where I was supposed to be despite any set back or lack of forward momentum. I was responsible to do my due diligence and to work as smartly and efficiently as I could with the gifts I had been given. First Corinthians 15:58 says, *"Therefore, my dear brothers and sisters, stand firm. Let nothing move you. Always give yourselves fully to the work of the Lord, because you know that your labor in the Lord is not in vain."* What a relief and joy to know that all I could do was the best I could do, and the rest was in my Heavenly Father's hands.

Maintaining Motivation in a Results-Driven World

It's tough to stay the course when we don't see results. Everything in our culture is focused on getting things done so we can reap the rewards. We have "to do" lists, but most of us do not have "to pray for" or "to meditate on" lists. We're inundated by messaging such as *Git 'er Done* and *Just Do It!* Colossians 3:23 goes on to say, *"Whatever you do, work at it with all your heart, as working for the Lord, not for human masters."* Boom. There it is again, the fount of our **Persistence**. Sometimes time and effort don't equal big results and we are frustrated and angry at God. Turn that frustration into faithfulness because God is at work in us whether we can see it or not. His timing is not our timing.

In 1 Kings 19:9-18, Elijah hides out in a cave as a failed prophet with a death sentence on his head. His fellow teammates have all been murdered. He has been anointed for a singular purpose which has hit some huge snares, to say the least. He is alone, frustrated, and scared. When we hit this point where everyone and everything has turned against us, we flail and look for great signs and events to let us know we will survive, but that's not where we'll replenish our **Persistence** pail. Step out of the cave and onto the mountain top. Just as Elijah experienced, God is in the whisper.[3]

There are so many remarkable stories of individuals who seemingly lost it all only to realize that they had found the secret to their breakthrough. Had they not persisted, we never would have heard of them. Edwin Perkins, who started Kool-Aid in Hastings, Nebraska originally created Fruit-Smack, a concentrated liquid soft drink. When he encountered problems with breakage and leakage while shipping, Perkins decided to dehydrate Fruit-Smack into what we now know as Kool-Aid becoming the first powered soft drink sold in stores. During the Depression, banks were closed, and workers were laid off, yet Kool-Aid sales continued to increase. Even though he was not a chemist, Perkins **persisted** until he found a better way. Perkins persisted even when it appeared Kool-Aid might not succeed.

In a sense, ignorance is bliss. There are times when we are called to a deep self-evaluation but it's not every day. We can't live that way. Fénelon puts it beautifully,

> *"It is the will of God that we should be ignorant, and to reason about the way is to waste time trifling along it. The safest and shortest course is to renounce, forget, and abandon the demands of self, and through faithfulness to God to think no longer of such demands. This is what commitment means: to get out of self and self-love in order to get into God."*

Don't Miss the Miracles

Whatever pushback you're going through, please be sure you don't miss the miracle. During my monthly book club discussion inside one of the Pennsylvania State Correctional Institutes (SCI), a dear brother in Christ had obviously heard enough of me complaining about what was not happening and said to me, *"Tracey, why don't you focus on what you have and not what you don't have."* Wow. I still feel his words impressed on my heart. Yes, indeed, why didn't I focus on the abundance of blessings shown to me every day? Albert Einstein reportedly said, *"There are only two ways to live your life: as though nothing is a miracle, or as though everything is a miracle."* I was so focused on the future, I missed everything happening in the present. As my one friend said, I was trying to outfly my guardian angels.

During one of my doctoral classes we were given an assignment to pick a fruit of the Spirit we'd like to focus and improve upon. As an attainment addict, mine was obviously going to be Contentment. Sure, I gave God thanks for the blessings in my life, but I was lacking in joy and peace. If I was so content, why was what I had never enough? Don't get me wrong, a healthy sense of discontent continually prods us to never stop growing or serving. However, there should be joy in this endless pursuit of perfection, not frustration.

I created a Contentment Journal where I ended each day reflecting on all the miracles, no matter how big or small, and listed them one by one. I made a daily goal of 25 so I could be sure to capture all the little "God Nods" that happened throughout the day. This process helped me to see just how God was showing up as my co-laborer and making things happen that I never could have dreamed of. It's going on around you too; you must be still and stay vigilant in seeing and acknowledging it.

Fueling Your Discipline

Ambition is the fuel that keeps us going. Without it, we sputter to a standstill. A life without purpose can stagnate, bore, and sometimes even be a little depressing for us. That's why we continually circle back to our **Singularity** to ensure we are not drifting or stagnating. To be ambitious doesn't necessarily mean that you need to set impossibly high goals, like climbing Mount Everest. It means setting your sights on an objective that stretches your potential a little, encourages you to become a better person, and gives you a sense of pride at the idea of accomplishing it.

One of my favorite parables in the Bible is the Parable of the Talents. This lesson was one I did not fully comprehend until later in life. Jesus tells the Parable of the Talents to his disciples. It appears in Matthew 25:14–30, and another version of the parable can be found in Luke 19:11–27. The story in Matthew unfolds as follows: A man goes away on a trip. Before he leaves, he entrusts money to his slaves. To the first he gives five talents, to the second he gives two talents, and to the third he gives a single talent. The first two slaves double their money; they give the original investment and their profit to their master when he returns. The third slave, however, buries his talent out in a field instead of trying to make a profit; he returns only the single talent when his master comes back. The master is pleased with the first two slaves, but he is dissatisfied with the third's actions. He reprimands this slave and casts him out into the darkness.

When I was younger, I thought the master's treatment of the third servant was harsh. The third servant was just playing it safe, right? Who could blame him for that? The problem is that we are not called to play it safe. We are called to be productive.

We are tasked with using all our health, wealth, time, and abilities to produce good works in this world to benefit our fellow men and women. The third servant was just plain old lazy and took the path of least resistance. He made no attempt to go out and produce any type of return for his master. We can't stop after stating what we are planning to do and we can't be afraid to take risks. We must demonstrate in action how we have used the gifts and talents we have been given and yes, each of us has a unique set of gifts specially coded for us. Trust me when I say there is something special that you, and only you, can do. Take that risk and work until it comes into full bloom. It will take work; like a caterpillar emerging from the cocoon. Anything worthwhile takes intense and persistent effort.

Build Your Spiritual Vigor

As a junior officer in the Air Force, I had a commander with the nickname of Dragon Lady. She was exactly what was needed to keep those fighter jets fully mission capable. She was known for a famous phrase: *"Follow up, follow up, follow up."* She insisted on it. Even though someone said they did something, you needed to trust them, but also to verify that the task was completed. While some would say this was micromanaging, the fact is anyone who is in a leadership role knows that the work is never done just because you assign it to someone. You must ensure it gets done and follow through. No matter how many times those crew chiefs had completed their pre-flight checklists, the Production Supervisor still had to review the work done and sign off on the aircraft forms before the pilot was dispatched to fly the jet.

Even in my company we have a two-person rule for tasks to ensure the job is done right. We review each other's emails and proposals for completeness. We check our bank statements to make sure our accountants are paying the correct bills at the right time. We count books before packing them to make sure the customer gets exactly what they ordered. Following up and managing the work required to execute the dream is part of fueling the greatness within. You can see in one of my all-time favorite reads, Michael Gerber's, *The E-Myth Revisited*, how we are all a blend of entrepreneur, manager, and technician. There are multiple pieces and processes to every endeavor you undertake. You need to know how to keep your finger on the pulse of all of them so you can work *on* your business and not just *in* your business.

The follow up you'll need is tied to **Persistence.** You are not only doing things; you must circle back and make sure they got done. Oswald Chambers referred to this as being spiritually vigorous saints. I am no stranger to heartache; however, I thought when I got more involved in Kingdom work, this might subside. I was wrong. God's work is never complete in us, and when we are weak, He is strong.[4] Hardships activate showers of grace and you never know what your values are until they are tested. Life is a contact sport, and you're going to get your nose bloodied again and again. The reason God lets adversity stay in our lives is so we can learn how to fight while relying on his power and in a manner reflecting the God seed within us.

Every successful person was once a greater failure than you've ever been (and may even still be). Say what? How can that be? The truth is they have failed so many times on their way to success, a comparison isn't even close. The more you persist, the more boulders you're going to have either gone around or smashed through. So why moan about it when our best-laid plans consistently fall apart? God isn't surprised by our failures. In fact, for some of us the only time we fall on our knees is right after we fall on our face! Lastly, no work will work unless it exalts God and his glory. So, don't expect miracles to happen unless those actions are tied directly to the God-directed fire burning inside of you.

You've got to fail now to get the glory later. Remember the tagline, *No guts, no glory?* It's a timeless truth no matter the generation or context. Small setbacks are the steppingstones for huge breakthroughs. Just talk to any successful person and they'll echo the same topsy-turvy, up again, down again, one day you're in and the next day you're out, mantra. Monty Hall said it best, *"I'm an overnight success; it just took twenty years."*

Eliminate Excess Baggage

If you're going to climb to the summit, you'll need to get rid of pre-conceived notions, naysayers, and negativity. You need to dislodge any bad habits. You'll also need to be hypervigilant about your schedule. Something has got to give as time and **Resources** are finite. We each only have 24 hours in a day and you've made the commitment to drive towards your singular purpose. You'll need to eliminate non-value-added tasks. In her book, *The Sales Messenger*, author and dear friend Mary Anne Wihbey-Davis shares a parable of a group of individuals who routinely got together to network. However, after years of gathering for breakfast they had to confront the cold, hard truth that nothing was happening. They enlisted the help of a mentor who made them color-code their daily activities. Anything that was not revenue generating was pushed off the calendar, including vacations. No results and no revenue meant no rest and no relaxation.

When I decided to go back for my doctorate in 2015, I made some important tradeoffs. I had to examine my schedule and push anything off my plate that would get in the way of my completion of a Ph.D. in four years. Some things I had to continue, like running the business, taking care of certain ministries, and personal fitness. However, there were other things I had to put aside for the next four years. These included watching television, the news, and social media; also coming off boards when my term was completed, and limiting attendance at social events. If I wanted to get this degree, I had to set myself up for success. When you put something new on your plate, something old must come off. Otherwise, you'll drop something or run the risk of burn out.

In my father's best-selling book, *Life is Tremendous*, he refers to his seven Laws of Leadership. One of them is titled "Production to Perfection". This law states, if you're not learning to make something happen today, you won't know much about perfection tomorrow. Or as another one of my heroes, General George S. Patton, said, *"A good plan violently executed now is better than a perfect plan executed next week."* Life contains a great deal of fog and friction. Most of the time we are flying blind in some aspect. All we can do is the best we can do. We'll never get it just right; we're not God! But in the process of producing results, we get closer and closer to perfection. Production to perfection through **Persistence** is about moving through what we *know* into the realm of *application*. We must literally live out our dreams in order to perfect them.

Finish strong; it will set the stage for where you land next. Remember the story of the tortoise and the hare. Slow but steady wins the race. Remember that you are a slingshot in the hands of life; you'll get stretched back and repositioned repeatedly, aching to launch and get some forward momentum. But that will only happen when the time is right, and you have the required target and momentum you need to hit the target. Until then, keep on keeping on and never, ever, ever, give up.

Pulling the Essentials Together

Singularity is born in your heart; **Persistence** is worked out with your hands. However, these two excellent qualities are not enough on their own. If all we needed to ignite the greatness within was self-contained, we wouldn't need each other as humanity and could survive and thrive as independent entities. Vision, courage, and hard work aren't enough to get us where we need to be. That's where so much of modern leadership material falls short. You've got yourself dialed in; but now it's time to flip the coin to the other side. In the next chapters we focus on what you need externally to bring out the best version of you!

Final Thoughts

This chapter focused on the price you'll pay, **Persistence**, to make your **Singularity** a reality. Never forget that God worked for six days before he rested. There is a glorious theology of work. In Genesis 1, we see that man was created to have dominion over fish, birds, livestock, and creatures on the ground; and to reproduce and subdue the Earth, even before the perfection of Eden was marred by sin. God created all kinds of work: redemptive, creative, providential, revelatory, justice, and compassionate. There is never a shortage of things requiring our effort and attention.

Many cite the book of Proverbs as the greatest leadership book of all time. I concur. It is filled with 31 chapters of how we are to interact with one another and spends a tremendous amount of time on the topic of work and the evils on non-work, using awesome descriptors such as sluggard, simple-ton, and slacker. One of the highest compliments you can give someone is to recognize their grit. I have always told my team-mates I was not concerned with the outcome if I knew we were giving it our all.

So now that you understand the two internal pieces you are responsible for—**Singularity** and **Persistence**—it's now time to flip the coin and recognize the external factors essential to ignite the greatness within.

Onto **Advocates**!

SP**A**RK

THREE

ADVOCATES: RECALIBRATE
YOUR TRIBE

"Be extremely distrustful of your intellect
and your own ideas of perfection."

—François Fénelon

Do you feel alone and isolated—like no one has your back? Do you look around and hear others speaking about their mentors and partners and feel envious of their connections? Is your pride secretly preventing you from asking for or accepting help when you need it the most? The cold hard truth is that a lone sheep is a dead sheep. This chapter is all about how to build a robust support network so you are never alone. A cord of three strands is not easily broken; the same goes for the human spirit. Read on and find out why you should never walk alone and never have to.

In the first two chapters we covered the internal items you'll need to accomplish through your own vision and grit. In the next three chapters we're going to cover the external equipment, starting with "A" for **Advocates**. **Advocates** are helpers, anointers, cheerleaders, ardent supporters, lifelong friends, colleagues, cohorts, prayer warriors, accountability partners, life coaches, healthy-habit mentors, truth tellers, and your core tribe. They're your wingmen and they'll never leave your side. No matter how strong or tenacious we are, we need at least one person in our corner otherwise we're toast. In short, you can't get it right without the fueling of **Advocates**.

There is a specific type of efficacy in leadership literature titled collective efficacy. Collective efficacy relates to how those in the group impact each other. The more confident and capable your **Advocates** or teammates, the higher your level of perceived self-efficacy. This relationship dynamic impacts the individual and increases the organizational efficacy as a whole. That's why successful people are surrounded by a host of even more successful people. Collective efficacy embodies the phrase "standing on the shoulders of giants." We gain and grow based on who we know.

The inspiration for this chapter came to me while watching a movie titled, *Darkest Hour*. The fate of Western Europe hung on Winston Churchill during the early days of World War II. The newly appointed British prime minister had to decide whether to negotiate with Hitler or fight on against incredible odds. There is a scene where Churchill is beaten down by all sides, internal as well as external, and is ready to negotiate with Mussolini because no one is **advocating** for him. The fate of Britain hangs on him and him alone; a terrible and impossible situation. Churchill is in his bedroom surrounded by darkness when King George comes to meet with him in his home. King George, after momentarily contemplating fleeing to live in exile in Canada, realizes that he must stay and fight; and that he must give Churchill his full support. That is exactly what the king does. In this scene, you can literally watch the air and blood return to Churchill's body and his face light up with new determination. You see, we don't need a whole army—sometimes just one other human being willing to fight alongside us for our success is all that's necessary.

Task or Relational

It took me many years to understand the power of **Advocates**. When I was younger, I dreamt of being an astronaut. The idea of launching into the vast, void of space appealed to me for some reason. I must also confess; I am really looking forward to working with robots because I think life will be so much easier and more efficient. Is there something wrong with me? Absolutely not. We live in a world that withers us. My father had a saying,

> *"My problem isn't keeping myself motivated, it's trying to keep other people from demotivating me!"*

Truer words were never spoken.

I have always considered myself emotionally engaging and socially savvy, however I have this strong pull to work alone and find solutions quickly. During my doctoral studies I discovered a free test online called the Least-Preferred Coworker (LPC). Go ahead and laugh; I'm still laughing and when I describe the test you'll understand why. This evaluation explained a lot about how I—and many others—are coded and why loners like us need to work to develop and maintain an indispensable communal network in order to keep fueling the greatness within. A **SPARK** dies out without propellant, and so will you.

The gist of the LPC test is to determine if you are more task or relationship oriented. Many of us have learned that working with others requires you to be a tremendous blend of both task and relationship; but we all have one side that we will tend to favor. In case you haven't guessed it, I tend toward the task focus. This grounding worked well with me in my former careers in the military, high tech, defense, and intelligence. We weren't there to make friends; we were there to get things done. It's important that you understand what types of people you resonate and work best with.

We taskers like concrete thinkers who get to the point. Relationship types will favor a more collective and emotive type of cohort. Neither is right or wrong, better or worse. Developing your self-awareness is the number one trait of emotional intelligence. We owe it to ourselves and others to find out how we tick and with whom we click. Context is also extremely important. In daily operations, we can be a productive and enjoyable mix of both task and relationship. In times of peace and prosperity, we can tip our relationship hats. When a crisis emerges, however, we'd better put our task boots on and get to work.

I bring up the LPC because there are those of us who are coded to be more loners than others. Truthfully, albeit humorous, Pee-wee Herman's line in the movie Pee-wee's Big Adventure, *"I'm a loner, Dottie. A rebel"*, always resonated with me. People are a paradox. They can make life worth living and then take it from us. Seems like this sentiment is a universal truth. King David wrote in Psalm 118:8, *"It is better to take refuge in the LORD than to trust in humans"* and the Apostle Paul wrote, when he was at his weakest point, he was strongest because he trusted in the Lord to get him through. Anyone who has put their trust in people knows that things do not always pan out the way you hope. Anyone who is honest with themselves also knows how they have repeatedly failed others.

Barbra Streisand has a hauntingly beautiful song whose lyrics go like this, *"People, people who need people, are the luckiest people in the world."* I can remember hearing this as a child and thinking that I couldn't wait to grow up and have these kinds of people in my life! After repeatedly investing my time and energy in the wrong individuals, however, I began wondering what in the world Babs was talking about. Who were these people and where were they? Was there a different planet filled with people who didn't hurt you and take advantage of you? So, what's going on?

Still, with all the miscommunication and pain, there's something synergistic that happens when two or more are gathered. We are not made to be alone.[1] We were never meant to be alone. The story of creation clearly shows that it is not good for us to be alone and God created a means for us to replicate so there could be more of us on the planet. He coded us for attachment because we all have the divine imprint as his sons and daughters. We are family. As God loves us, we are to love each other, and that means we are relationally coded. Ecclesiastes 4:9-12 has a beautiful description of unity and the image of a cord:

> *Two are better than one, because they have a good return for their labor: If either of them falls down, one can help the other up.*
> *But pity anyone who falls and has no one to help them up. Also, if two lie down together, they will keep warm. But how can one keep warm alone?*
> *Though one may be overpowered, two can defend themselves. A cord of three strands is not quickly broken.*

Our goal as a singular race is to bring the body together. I heard an incredible pastor in downtown Pittsburgh exclaim during a Sunday church service, *"There is only one race! The human race!"* The diverse congregation went wild with cheers. We are to bring the body together. Life in the Spirit is about fellowship, community, and collaboration, yet we have an epidemic of loneliness, hopelessness, and divisiveness. That's because we have not yet realized the importance of **Advocates** in our lives. We simply can't get from here to there without help.

Whenever I learn of someone going through one of life's trials or betrayals, I immediately ask, "Who is their support system?" It is amazing the number of times the person sharing the news with me says, "They don't have anyone." This is like going through life without insurance or sailing off into a body of water without a life vest. It's not a matter of if you are going to die, but when. It's not a matter of if someone is going to betray you or turn your life into a crisis, but when. Just as we don't rely on someone else to purchase insurance for us, we'd better get to work on assembling the most authentic, loyal, and wise **Advocates** to surround us and form the fibers in our weave of life's network.

"One line delivered at the right time, received with a tender heart, can open the flood gates of Heaven above and give someone a brand-new start." Tracey C. Jones

Are You With Me or Against Me?

We are more virtually connected than ever and yet more emotionally separated. Social media is often anything but social. The real issue isn't that we don't have people in our lives, it's that we don't have the right people in our lives. We have contacts, connections, and associates we may count as friends. In all reality, these types of individuals often barely register on the spectrum of acquaintances. This assortment of pseudo-**Advocates** may not be there when the inevitable fires of life ignite. Their threads of "friendship" may melt and fall away at the first sign of heat.

There is no doubt that God places and uses people in our lives at very special times and for very specific reasons. That's why when we begin to pull away from others and isolate ourselves, we become like a bird in a gilded cage; it may be comfortable, but it is constraining and it will imprison you right out of the land of the living. This regression is the beginning of a dangerous spiral. As you are going through this book's contents, think about who you will have in your corner alongside you as you ignite your inner **spark**. Remember, greatness and isolation are mutually exclusive. You can have one or the other—not both. We need others to bring out our innate greatness.

Several years ago, I went through yet another bout of, "I can't believe what those closest to me did!" Only this time, I was done—with everyone—forever. I may be good at some things in life, but I was a miserable failure at picking those who I needed in my tribe. I was ready to go full-on modern hermit and stay at home with my books, and my dogs, puttering around in my garden, writing, researching, and living happily ever after—alone. How could I go out and live a tremendous life when I didn't see much tremendous about it? I was supposed to love people.....*but people were dragging me down!* People who bit the hand that fed them! I was played, betrayed, and full of rage. I felt like the children's song, *"Nobody likes me, everybody hates me, I think I'll go eat worms."* This will happen to each of us, so just remember; bitterness and heartache push you in one of two directions. You can either go the path of separation and choose to check out, or you can strive towards restoration and find a path forward through healing and redemption.

After climbing out of my pity pit, I wiped the tears from my eyes, looked up, and saw a book on my desk (imagine that). It must have been a sample copy sent to me by a publisher and the Holy Spirit instructed me to crack the cover—now. I wasn't dialed into the Spirit's voice at that time in my life and now see this supernatural nudge as providence. I obeyed. I have found that whenever I am in a rut, or despondent, or screwed up so badly I can't even talk to anyone, the best course of action is to reach for a book. This one was titled, *The Power of the Other*, by one of my favorite authors, Dr. Henry Cloud. This book literally saved me from my vow of solitude and brought me back into the land of the living. Dr. Cloud outlines four relational quadrants. The goal is to draw down or limit your exposure to individuals you are connected to in the first three quadrants so you can put emphasis on the fourth one. I'm not going to discuss the first three groups of people because I want you to get that book and read it for yourself. You will not be disappointed.

The fourth group of individuals Dr. Cloud details are those who are your staunchest supporters. They have your back and want your success even more than you want it. They are more than mentors; they provide you with the necessary fuel and support for your ownership and success. They push us to new limits while helping us process failure in a meaningful way. In short, they'd take a bullet for us and would charge up any hill by our side. Then it hit me, I had many *others* in my life, I just didn't have enough quadrant four people in my tremendous tribe. Just as we have to constantly be revisiting our activities in seeing **Singularity** and pursuing **Persistence,** it is critical for us to take stock of who we have in our lives on a recurring basis. Not all relationships are created equal. People are the cause of our heartaches, but they are also the solution to them. We need a keen mind to assess which side of the fence every-one who crosses our paths is on.

Advocates Talk to People

The Greek word for the gift of prophecy is *propheteia* which is the ability to receive a divinely inspired message and deliver it to others in the church. The gift of prophecy is a supernatural gift of the Holy Spirit whereby the individual receives input and is directed to dispense that which was given. Paul says in 1 Corinthians 14:1 to *"Follow the way of love, and eagerly desire gifts of the spirit, especially prophesy."* So according to Paul, prophecy is the greatest gift. I used to think the gift of prophesy was not valid anymore and was a product of Old Testament prophets speaking directly with God and coming down from the mount announcing, "Thus sayeth God!" Well, that was then and this is now; and the gift of Prophecy is more alive than ever. How? In the New Testament, apostles took over the role from the Prophets and in the Age of the Church, this gift falls to any believer who receives this gifting and uses it for the good of all and those words are to be tested for truth against Scriptural standards.

One of the greatest traits of leadership, or any human endeavor for that matter, is wisdom. In layman's terms we call it discernment. In my experience, prophecy is spiritual discernment and we need people in our lives who will give us a divinely inspired word when we need it the most. These messages can take the form of exhortation, correction, rebuke of secret sins, prediction of future events, edification, comfort, and inspiration. Their words equip and edify you, not pacify and appease you. The spiritual **Advocate** will be so dialed into the gifting of the Holy Spirit that they will be able to relay a human interpretation of the revelations they received after they have been given.

You may cross paths with a powerful **Advocate** in a chance meeting. These seemingly random acts of kindness can lead to a life of purposefulness. Numerous individuals ordained by God crossed my path for a brief minute, sharing only a word or two. I have also experienced the reverse when people were physically placed in front of me and the Lord laid it on my heart to share a word with them. Every time there is an open seat beside me at an event I either ask the person if I may move over and sit next to them or ask them to move next to me. I once asked a couple how they met and the husband explained that while in an airport in the Midwest, a woman came up to him and told him he would meet his wife at work. He had been there for years so this was difficult to process. Then, the women who became his wife attended a work function where their paths intersected and they entered the covenant of marriage. The woman who spoke to him was using the gift of Prophecy and my friend was open to receive. Even if you don't care for what your **Advocate** is dispensing, always remain an open vessel to receive their wisdom. There is a definitive reason they came across your path.

Advocates Walk With People

You need to surround yourself with people who are going to physically walk with you as accountability partners. The Bible is clear that our enemy moves about like a roaring lion waiting to pounce and devour us.[2] Whenever I hear of someone's fall from grace I immediately think, where was their support structure? Who saw what was happening (and believe me, somebody always knows) and allowed this kind of behavior, thoughts, attitude, or decision making to go on? Never forget, God shows up in people because he is *in* people. If you isolate yourself from truth tellers, or surround yourself with yes people or negative people, you are in dire trouble! As I mentioned in the author's note, my father always told me, *"Only an honest man can realize how dishonest he his."* Seeing as we like to tell ourselves all kinds of comforting lies, we best have **Advocates** on speed dial. A true **Advocate** can already sense that your fire is getting quenched and will quickly advise you on how to get your flame back and burning brightly.

The devil loves to get you isolated or under poor leadership or false friendships; he is the great deceiver and roaring lion. But remember, no one ever died from the roar of a lion. All he can do is sow fear, whisper doubt, and cause conflict. Do not allow this unholy entity any space in your head, heart, or spirit. Always remember, if you are not talking to God, you are talking to Satan and giving him top secret classified intelligence about where to attack next. When you're alone is when you're most vulnerable. True **Advocates** remind us that although we have moral agency or free will, there are always consequences, both good and bad. They'll make you think before you act, consider the big picture, and stop you dead in your tracks before you completely derail. If they don't, they don't need to be in your life.

Most of us can't change our life on our own. We need someone to act as a guide or a mentor. If you've been stuck in the same old rut for years and years and still have not gotten serious about getting real help in your life to help you make the change you need, I tell you with love in my heart that you just don't care enough. You'll never achieve greatness until you get serious about attacking and stripping away the negative, evil, useless, or non-God honoring aspects of or people in your life. On the flip side, steer clear of pouring your efforts into those who don't want to use the gifts of counsel or **Resources** you are offering them. "Do not throw your pearls to pigs".[3]

The Chosen Few

As we gain our first steps of independence in building friendships, most of us show a tendency to have a large group of friends in our lives. That *need* of such a large group is rooted in insecurity. The truth is we don't need, and can't adequately manage, a large group of friends. We need a couple of authentic ones in our inner circle. Jesus was closer to some of his followers than to others. He had many disciples, twelve apostles and an inner circle of three best friends: Peter, James and his beloved disciple, John. He shared some things with all of his followers and more personal things with the apostles—for instance at the Last Supper—but he reserved his most intimate moments for his inner circle.

Jesus shared with these three closest friends his most glorious moments, like his Transfiguration[4] and his most painful moments, like the agony in the garden[5]. These three were the ones who knew Jesus the best and the price he was paying personally to do his Father's will. These three knew more than the others who Jesus was on the inside. They knew more about his courage, as well as his fears. I have one key **Advocate** for each major area of my life: personal, financial, professional, spiritual, and physical. That way I can utilize the gifting of a core group of experts, rather than draining a singular resource. No one person can do it all for you; so, build up your cadre of committed **Advocates**. Think of this core group as the board of directors in your life. They are there to support you with sage wisdom, encouragement, and connections. These individuals will save you time, money, and heartache and pour blessings into your life.

Let me give you an example of this. My father received the prestigious Cavett Award in 2006. This award is the highest honor the membership of the National Speakers Association can bestow on a peer. Cavett Robert was the co-founder of the National Speakers Association and a dear friend of my father. My father received a glorious statue of Cavett speaking, which is proudly displayed in my home, and a plaque which had pictures of the people in his life who were instrumental in building him up to become the world-renowned internationally acclaimed speaker he was. This listed included: Gloria, his wife who he referred to as "My Everything", George Mowery, his Sunday School Teacher who he referred to as "My Role Model", the Reverend Tracy C Miller, his pastor and my namesake who my father referred to as "My Teacher", Cavett Robert, who my father called "My Dear Friend", Willard Neisen, who he referred to as "My Book Mentor", and Deacon Jones, his earthly father who he referred to as "My Hero". These are the individuals that ignited and fueled my father's tremendous life. Find your tremendous tribe and keep them close. Have them each fill a critical area so you can live a fully integrated and congruent life.

Advocates Are Your Backbone

Proverbs 13:20 states, *"Walk with the wise and become wise, for a companion of fools suffers harm."* **Advocates** tell you when to stand firm. Moses is the most powerful prophet in the Bible. There were many prophets, but only one Moses. Almost everyone on this planet can cite Moses' most impressive miracle as the time when he parted the waters of the Red Sea so that his people, the Israelites, could escape their pursuing captors, the Egyptians. Moses tells his people to "stand firm and see the deliverance of the Lord"; although the people vocally doubted why they were even delivered only to die outside their current homes. *Moses answered the people, "Do not be afraid. Stand firm and you will see the deliverance the LORD will bring you today. The Egyptians you see today you will never see again. The LORD will fight for you; you need only to be still."*[6] **Advocates** will use their power to shield you and come to your rescue.

Advocates are Few and Far Between

We all have this false assumption that we need to be doing all kinds of things with a bevy of bystanders. Having a large group around us doesn't necessarily mean they are true **Advocates**. The larger our network the more powerful our influence, however, relationships are about quality, not quantity. The thinner we spread ourselves relationally, the more diluted our bonds become. In his book, *Talking with God*, French theologian François Fénelon, writes, *"It is indeed good to see only the friends whom God gives us, and to be protected from all the rest!"* He tells us to seek a certain number of people who can refresh our mind and spirit when we *are in need of it*. One quick test to see if someone is an **Advocate** or an albatross (no offense to albatrosses) is this: after 15 minutes with this individual do you feel refreshed or drained? You can feel it inside. This may have nothing to do with the content of the conversation but rather the motives of the communicator. I've had some really heavy conversations with great minds that left me feeling like I could conquer the world. On the flip side, I've gotten sucked into a black hole of nonsense with petty spirits and biting tongues so nasty that I felt like I needed a shower to get rid of the filth they spewed or regurgitated. Pay close attention to the pings of the Holy Spirit on your conscience during conversations and cut short the wasted breath of negative spirits.

If you allow yourself to continue in constant interactions that could be avoided with people of this nature, you are setting barriers between yourself and your progress.

We need **Advocates** to tell us to shut up and quit sucking our thumbs! My father used to bring audiences to tears of laughter joking about all the thumb suckers he had to endure. **Advocates** will form a quorum. It will be seconded. **Advocates** will give correction in such a way that you are able to absorb it. **Advocates** help people be honest with themselves. They don't shirk their responsibility to tell you the truth. In 2 Samuel 12, there's a brilliant exchange whereby Nathan rebukes King David. Rather than directly pointing out the King's faults, Nathan uses a parable to illustrate the wrongness of what David has himself done, finally exclaiming, "You are the man!"

Advocates are Cheerleaders

We are coded for attachment. We need cheerleaders in our lives. Our existence depends on our supporters. Dan McAdams said,

> *"Our very survival depends on the effective social commitments of hardworking, caring, and emotionally stable adults who need to step up to the plate, in the prime of their lives, and take on the most daunting adaptive challenges that face the group."*

We must be self-motivated; however, we can never lose sight of the importance of others in motivating us. Our mentors serve as role models. Paul, sends his mentee, Timothy, to serve as an **Advocate** in his absence;

> *"Therefore, I urge you to imitate me. For this reason, I have sent to you Timothy, my son whom I love, who is*

faithful in the Lord. He will remind you of my way of life in Christ Jesus, which agrees with what I teach everywhere in every church".[7]

My father used to say,

"Hang around thinkers; you'll be a better thinker. Hang around givers; you'll be a better giver. Hang around workers; you'll be a better worker. Hang around a bunch of thumb sucking, complaining, griping boneheads; and you will be a better thumb sucking, complaining, griping bonehead."

Advocates need to be pouring into us and raising us up to their level of attitude and performance.

Would it surprise you if I told you that many of my staunchest **Advocates** were behind bars? As I mentioned earlier, I conduct monthly book discussions in three state correctional institutions in my home state of Pennsylvania. We've been together for years reading, sharing, thinking, worshipping, and growing. Some of the sagest advice I have ever received has come from these brothers. They have a way of cutting through the niceties and nonsense to tell me what I need to hear right then and there. After all, if they don't say it then, I don't get the chance to interact with them for another thirty days, and that can go longer depending on what is going on in the prison such as a lockdown or lack of volunteer support.

They also know I'm *their* biggest **Advocate**. If you ever want to feel valued, do prison ministry. These men know we get paid nothing to visit them and do this solely because we love and value them. We see the greatness inside. Many of them have had family members who have tired of going back year after year. Their lives continue on the outside while these men must finish out theirs on the inside. These men understand the criticality of **Advocates** in their lives. In fact, many of them wound up in prison because of unregenerate friends or as it says in Romans 1:28, they hung around those with a reprobate mind. Proverbs 11:14 says, *"For lack of guidance a nation falls, but victory is won through many advisers."*

Wisely Discern Your Advocates

As stated above, the Apostle Paul clearly states that if you are hanging out with reprobates, you need to stop immediately. You are only blocking the blessing pipeline by staying in the company of people who do not share acknowledgement of the divine nature. Think back, if you're honest with yourself, we've all been there. Fénelon says even the best intentioned of these will lead us astray. *"They may be good, honest, faithful, and they may have all those qualities which make friendship perfect in the eye of the world, but for us they are infected, and their good-naturedness only makes them more dangerous."* That's not a very popular stand in our blind tolerance and open-ended love preaching world. But, that doesn't make it any less true.

There are 18 inches between a pat on the back and a kick in the rear. You must pick people who can deliver both and work hard to keep them committed to your inner circle. Jesus chastised Peter in Matthew 16:23 in a harsh manner calling him a stumbling block and accusing him of human, and not Godly, concerns. Ouch! **Advocates** will check you. They'll stop you from doing a good thing so you can do a great thing. One last word of advice, it's easy to idolize our **Advocates**. But please remember, though your **Advocates** are sent by God, but they are not God; so, don't mistake them for God. They can provide wise counsel, but you always need to go before the Lord for the ultimate seal of approval.

The Greatest Advocate of All

There is only one relationship based on unconditional love. Every other relationship we have in our lives ebbs and flows based on what the other person promises and delivers. Even our staunchest **Advocates** and closest blood relatives will fail us. We are incapable of giving love or accepting love unconditionally. But there is one who is—God—and there is proof. The proof is that God gave his own Son, the most precious, single, possession in the entire cosmos, in order to adopt us into his family and when Jesus departed this earth, he delivered another in his place, the Holy Spirit, to serve as our **Advocate** and helper.

The Holy Spirit's current role is the indwelling of believers and abiding with them forever (John 14:16). This spiritual indwelling grants supernatural degrees of self-efficacy. One of Jesus' last earthly promises was to send the Holy Spirit to the Apostles. In Acts 2:2-4, the Holy Spirit came like the blowing of a violent wind from heaven upon the disciples at the day of Pentecost. That same Spirit is not only with us—but within us—today.

Before you can ignite the greatness within, you've got to recognize and acknowledge there is greatness within, if you will just open the door. Burning with a white-hot flame requires a different type of fire. White flames are considered the hottest burning fires and can reach temperatures of 2,500 to 2,900 degrees Fahrenheit. If you're going to burn, you've got to burn hot, baby! No weak flame or tepid temperature will do. That's an exact description of the indwelling of the Holy Spirit who baptizes us with fire (Luke 24:49, Acts 1:4, Acts 1:8, 1 Cor. 12:1-31).

What's consuming you? Is it the spirit of greed? The spirit of revenge? The spirit of fear and loneliness? Or is it the Holy Spirit? First Corinthians 12 outlines the gifts of the Holy Spirit. These gifts are turbo-charged premiums freely given to us as part of our inheritance. You want to claim your eternal inheritance now in this earthy realm? All you must do is ask. The greatest thing you can do for yourself in igniting the greatness within is to not quench the power of the Holy Spirit (1Thess. 5:19), but rather allow the power within you to blaze.

Fear and Revere

There are times when we need to act and do not need to confer with flesh. When we get the prompting of the Holy Spirit, we must not delay, protest, or debate, but rather steadily obey. In these cases, seeking outside counsel is used strictly to talk one-self out of doing what one needs to do. Much of what ails us is because of our failure to act. We know what the root cause of our issue is, and it is our responsibility to remedy the situation through immediate action.

The Holy Spirit is the greatest **Advocate** of all. He inter-cedes for us. He speaks when we cannot. He is constantly in touch with the Father on our behalf. He is our dearest friend and we can grieve him. So, don't. You wouldn't intentionally break your best friend's, spouses or mother's heart. The Spirit is the truest source to igniting the greatness within. Greatness is already burning in you; just don't douse it or put it out.

Advocates are life's greatest blessing. Be open to their wis-dom. Be wise in who you allow in your inner circle. When

Jesus' teachings were too hard for many of his followers to hear they turned and walked away. When Christ asked Simon Peter if he would leave too, Simon Peter replied, "Lord, to whom shall we go?".[8] If you are running low on fuel it's time to find another power supply—the one true power supply that contains the words of eternal life and be ready to pour into another's life when a word is given or a situation arises. No one is meant to go it alone. We need to be as intentional about cultivating our tremendous tribe as we are about our other important life decisions.

Final Thoughts

Proverbs 11:14 stresses the importance of and safety found in wise counsel. We were never meant to shoulder life's burdens alone. Yet in our pride, we feel we possess everything within ourselves to meet daily demands and counter future forces. The greatest men and women throughout history had their special core around them who ministered to them in incredibly unique and sustaining ways.

For some of us reaching out for a hand up is quite natural; while for others, it's a sign of weakness or lack of ability. But my prayer is that you are keenly aware of the multitude of **Advocates** surrounding you. They say God doesn't call the qualified; he qualifies the called. And that is always accomplished by the words, actions, wisdom, prayer, and resources of **Advocates**.

Onto **Resources!**

SPARK

FOUR

RESOURCES: RECALIBRATE
YOUR SUPPLIES

"When you believe in your dream and your vision,
then it begins to attract its own resources.
No one was born to be a failure."

—Myles Munroe

"There is really no true charity except that which
will help others to help themselves, and place
within the reach of the aspiring the means to climb."

—Andrew Carnegie

"I want you to bear in mind that your text books, with
all their contents, are not an end, but a means to an end,
a means to help us get the highest, the best, the purest
and the most beautiful things out of life."

—Booker T. Washington

Do you feel frustrated—like a slingshot that keeps getting pulled backwards when all you want to do is launch? Can you see where you want to go, but lack the means to get there? Are you able to accurately assess what's needed to move forward and what's holding you back that you need to eject? This chapter is all about discovering the **Resources** you need to get the job done right. As we learned in the previous chapter, none of us are meant to go it alone. Community is a core keystone habit and once you have identified the right people, processes, and provisions, you'll be on your way!

How to Cross a River

Three Air Force Officers were walking through the woods and suddenly they found themselves standing in front of a huge, wild river. They desperately had to get to the other side, but how with such a raging torrent? The first Officer knelt down and prayed to the Lord: "Lord, please give me the strength to cross this river!"
Poof!
The Lord gave him long arms and strong legs. Now he could swim across the river. It took him about two hours and he almost drowned several times. BUT he was successful!
The second Officer, who observed this, prayed to the Lord and said: "Lord, please give me the strength AND the necessary tools to cross this river!"
Poof!
The Lord gave him a tub and he managed to cross the river, despite the fact that the tub almost capsized a couple of times.
The third Officer who observed all this knelt down and prayed: "Lord, please give me the strength, the means and the intelligence to cross this river!"
Poof!
The Lord converted the Officer into a Sergeant. The Sergeant took a quick glance on the map, walked a few meters upstream and crossed the bridge.

Calling in the Calvary

"The cavalry" is an often-used metaphor referring to the quickest or strongest means of resolving a situation (in one's favor). The phrase refers to a military squadron or dragoons, who were soldiers that fought on horseback in years gone by. Anyone who's done a home improvement project knows you can't get the job done right without the right tools. Sometimes you'll need brawn, sometimes gadgets, and other times, brains. This chapter is all about identifying the **Resources** you need so you can procure them and get to work. You can have all the vision, drive, and support in the world, but without the right people, processes, and pieces, you won't gain any of the traction required for sustaining forward momentum. So, if you're feeling frustrated because the effort and money you're investing is evaporating into a whole lotta nothing, read this chapter carefully.

There's a specific type of self-efficacy in leadership literature known as, *means efficacy*. Means efficacy is defined as the means and/or **Resources** available to human agents (i.e. us) to perform tasks. These **Resources** must be considered when examining an individual's or group's perceived capability and subsequent motivation to perform. Means efficacy therefore "results from perceptions of an enabling and supportive context".[1] If you've ever said to yourself, "If only I had the means I could accomplish this task" you know exactly what I'm talking about.

What this *means* is that while it's important to encourage people and help them gain clarity on their end goal, in jobs or situations that involve heavy use of internal processes or external materials, evidence is beginning to indicate that giving employees the means to be productive, means efficacy, may even overshadow self-efficacy in determining performance.[2] Hence, an enabling construct (means) for the follower may result in greater levels of organizational effectiveness than self-efficacy alone. In layman speak; *"I can't do the job without the tools for the job."*

Great Man theorist Thomas Carlyle (1840) also echoes this precursor to engagement stating, *"Man is a tool-using animal. Nowhere do you find him without tools; without tools he is nothing, with tools he is all."* Tools create the solutions needed to solve problems and create opportunity. In the Life-Changing Classic, *Maxims of Life and Business*, John Wanamaker writes, *"All business grows by what they have given to them."* No entity can survive, let alone thrive, without **Resources** or means being given to them. I can take the ship so far, but I cannot cross the ocean, let alone leave port, on my own.

You Can't Get it Right Without the Right People

In his article, *What Leaders Really Do*, John P. Kotter remarks that *"strong leadership with weak management is no better, and is sometimes actually worse, than the reverse"*. We sure put a lot of emphasis on leaders, but the truth is that leaders are nothing without technicians and executors in all areas of expertise. When I was in the Air Force, it took various types of maintenance personnel to launch, recover, and fix the squadrons' fighter jets: avionics personnel, crew chiefs, weapons loaders, and fuel and supply logisticians.

There cannot be a leader without followers; however, there may be followers without a leader. Leadership may land the big fish, but management cooks the creative dish. While the challenge is to have both, if you must settle for just one, pick management. Once the starting bell has rung, it is up to management to run the race by establishing organizational requirements and structures to accomplish the overarching vision and plan. Managers are the ones to draw up the tactical plans that will achieve the strategic goals and to determine what **Resources** they need to make the organizational goals successful. First Corinthians 9:24 states, *"Do you not know that in a race all the runners run, but only one gets the prize? Run in such a way as to get the prize"*. Our Lord has set our desired future, now it is up to us to be obedient in our day to day journey (**Persistence**).

Having a leader who sets the direction is critical (**Singularity**), however, you can't get it right without the right people doing the right things at the right times. It will be those people who will pull all the necessary ingredients together to deliver an organizational feast. Point leaders need point people and a visionary needs people who will put the vision into practice. Leaders need team members whom they don't just trust, but to whom they can *entrust*. These individuals are the ones who leaders can hand the keys to the kingdom knowing full well their followers will act as if the riches were their own. According to leadership expert Warren Bennis, *"Management is getting people to do what needs to be done."* That does not entail babysitting adults. Leaders need followers who are self-directed and have the integrity and common sense to do what needs to be done without having to be told every step of the way. Rodney Dangerfield said it best, *"Men who do things without being told draw the most wages."*

A leader can't transform without a solid team ready, willing, and eager to perform and you can't fuel the intrinsic **spark** within you without the necessary **resources**. Managers make things happen. The fact is, no solitary leader, no matter how charismatic and visionary, can single-handedly lead an organization of any size. It takes managers at all levels who translate the leader's desires into something the organization can sink its teeth into. The Christian walk is all about maintaining our joy amidst the drudgery as well as when trials befall us. So too is the critical role of a manager. Without them nothing would get done, no matter how brilliant or benevolent the leader.

Finding Exemplary Followers

One of the most humbling things for a leader to realize is that they cannot get to 'mission accomplished' as a solo act. The very definition of leadership is *"that which influences emergent social dynamics in such a way that organization members pride each other with purpose, motivation, and direction to achieve adaptive responses to challenges"*.[3] You'll need people in all levels of your organization who are teachable and adaptable. In my book, *A Message to Millennials*, I go into the seven functions of followership that leaders can use to target and train exemplary followers, otherwise known as co-leaders.

During my dissertation research I got burned out hearing about all the things leaders had to do. I had worked hard as a leader for decades but surely there was more to leadership than just placing all of the burden on the person at the top. After all, aren't we all supposed to be in this mission thing together? Well there is more—much, much more. The field of followership is a rich area of emerging focus in leadership literature. So rich, it was one of the areas I focused on in my dissertation. I came across a book that described the two key elements leaders need to watch for and cultivate in their team. Robert Kelley describes these two axes in his book, *The Power of Followership*.

First, each member must be a critical thinker. This means they can provide valuable input, come to solutions on their own, and possess the self-regulation to follow the rules and make ethical decisions. A critical mind is a far cry from a critical spirit. I've had team members who would willfully disobey or outright tell me "no". That is not critical thinking; that's insubordination. The second characteristic of the right people is "all in" engagement. This means they are "all in" for the mission and are not focused on what they can get out of it. These folks aren't just your early adopters, they are your co-leaders who will ensure everyone who isn't "all in" sees the value in where the organization is going. If you do not have fully engaged, critical thinking employees, you cannot get to where you need to go. Trust me. I've coached, cajoled, rewarded, bonused, and coddled many employees in an attempt to bring out the best in them only to see them become more entrenched in doing their own thing, and not the organization's.

Leader-Member Exchange (LMX) Theory

The fact is, however, the best in them may not be what's best for the organization. This is a very important truth you need to take the time to digest. It is also why some folks cannot and will not ever allow themselves to be completely and wholly brought on board. It's imperative that you come to an agreement about where *they* see themselves in the organization and where *you* see them in the organization post haste. If these two perspectives are not congruent, you need to find the right person for that seat. Please don't wait hoping things will get better. I hear so many well-meaning coaches explaining that if people just understood their role in the bigger picture, they'd come onboard. Hogwash. We are selfish by nature. It takes work to look beyond yourself to the greater good. My favorite leadership theory is called LMX which stands for leader-member exchange. Leadership is a dance, and it only works when both partners are working in unison and are willing to do their collective parts and it ain't dancing if one of you is dragging your feet or fighting the other's lead.

*Compensation may drive compliance, but
only cooperation yields commitment.*

The unique relationship between leaders worth following and follower's worth engaging emerged with the theory of Leader-Member Exchange (LMX), which developed increasing and organizationally enhanced levels of interaction between the leader and the individual follower.[4] In industrial and organizational psychology, an organizational citizenship behavior, or OCB, is an individual's voluntary commitment within an organization or company that is not part of his or her contractual tasks.[5] Organizational citizenship behavior has been studied since the late 1970s and is a key component of LMX Theory. Another name for LMX theory is the Vertical Dyad Linkage Theory, or VDL, which refers to the connections between the two, the leader and follower, and the degree of support given between the two.[6]

Those individuals who exhibit the flip side of tremendous OCBs are what I refer to as, SOBs, which stands for Self-Oriented Behaviors. These "followers" only follow themselves. They are not concerned about being a good organizational citizen. Their needs supersede the needs of the organization. Because of their unwillingness to be led, they create a tremendous amount of friction and drain **Resources** that are needed to keep the collective moving forward. Remember earlier when I referred to two types of individuals: orchids and dandelions? These folks are the orchids. They are always one request away from folding up and dying on the vine.

Hire the Inspired Because It's a Whole Lot Tougher to Inspire the Hired

As I stated earlier, you can't get it right without the right people, so make sure you find the right person for your needs. Not just anyone will do. When I transitioned from operating large bureaucratic organizations to running a small business, I had to look for a vastly different type of individual; someone who was able to work outside the constraints of layers of processes and be able to create and self-direct without constant feedback or oversight. I repeatedly put out job bids and hired employee after employee, but my success rate in finding the right fit was abysmal.

Finally, I let go of the *need to hire* desire and let God fill the slot. I literally stopped looking and allowed the individual to come to me to inspire their hire. I learned to trust my instincts rather than words on a resume. I hired with purpose, rather than out of pain. Too often, I would overlook shortcomings by rationalizing that I could train people. The problem is that you can't train for character or drive. You don't need to take these dead-end detours because God won't put you in a position with a job to do without surrounding you with the right people. If they haven't arrived yet; they will. You must be patient and not jump the gun. Your job is to simply make sure you have the need defined and to make sure you aren't blocking the blessing pipeline. They say when the student is ready the teacher will appear. I take it one step further and say that when the business is ready, the team member(s)/co-leader(s) will arrive.

You Can't Get it Right Without the Right Tools

Below is one of my all-time favorite jokes, mainly because it has such a powerful lesson. When you need assistance, and we all will in our lives, you must be open to asking for or receiving help. You must be willing and open to accept grace, mercy, donations, counsel, a loaner car, a place to stay until you get on your feet, any type of help. If you will not, this is a sign that your ego needs to be severely crushed. Better do it now before you are pruned to the quick.

A storm descends on a small town, and the downpour soon turns into a flood. As the waters rise, the local preacher kneels in prayer on the church porch, surrounded by water. By and by, one of the townsfolk rowed up the street in a canoe.

"Better get in, Preacher. The waters are rising fast."

"No," says the preacher. "I have faith in the Lord. He will save me."

Still the waters rise. The preacher is up on the balcony, wringing his hands in supplication, when another man zips up in a motorboat.

"Come on, Preacher. We need to get you out of here. The levee's gonna break any minute."

Once again, the preacher is unmoved. "I shall remain. The Lord will see me through."

After a while the levee breaks, and the flood rushes over the church until only the steeple remains above water. The preacher has cautiously climbed up as the waters continue to rise and is clinging to the cross when a helicopter descends out of the clouds, a state trooper calls down to him through a megaphone.

"Grab the ladder, Preacher. This is your last chance."

Once again, the preacher insists the Lord will deliver him.

And, predictably, he drowns.

A pious man, the preacher goes to heaven. After a while he gets an interview with God, and he asks the Almighty, "Lord, I had unwavering faith in you. Why didn't you deliver me from that flood?"
God shakes his head. "What else did you want from me? I sent you two boats and a helicopter."

Be Clear on Needs, not Wants

The next thing you must do in order to ignite your innate great is to take the time and figure out exactly what **Resources** you need to bring your vision to reality. Hope and prayer are only going to get you so far. You need hammers you can swing and plans you can build on. Perhaps it's a new marketing strategy, website, or a sales funnel; maybe it's an updated CRM database or a review of existing suppliers. Maybe you even need a better office location or perhaps you need only a virtual presence and can sell off expensive facilities. The point is business changes at the speed of light. You need to constantly monitor what you can keep in house and what you can outsource. Remember Michael Gerber's best-selling book, *The E-Myth Revisited*, extolling entrepreneurs to work *on* their business and not just *in* their business? Truer words were never spoken. That's why your team is so critical to aiding you in leading. They'll see things at their level that you won't at yours because you are responsible for looking outward—for example, new tools, new techniques, and new training that will help them bring the entity to the next level. Find out what it is they need (the means) and get it for them.

Data is the new currency; the speed at which we can translate data and distill and apply it is critical. Why are CEOs reluctant to invest? Margins? Immediacy of next quarter results? Interest rates? We need to look long term and invest in the **Resources** that are going to get us further than the next quarter's results. If you don't adopt a longer strategy you open the door to disruption from the outside. We are in a connected world. Use your **Resources** wisely. Businesses need to also be on the lookout for fragmentation. This is when players or competitors enter your revenue or donor stream by finding more effective ways of delivering some of the same solutions you do. I experience this every day in the logistics and publishing world. You may have a lock on a process or solution today, but tomorrow you may have a slice of your pie taken off your plate.

I recently heard a successful wealth planner muse about the location of the next group of emerging wealth. His insight was that the healthy will be wealthy because they will live the longest and will have the most years to amass the most wealth. We need to meet emerging needs for new clients. Find the emerging markets. How do we ensure we are able to meet the needs of our clients? Only 35 percent of the population find independence and entrepreneurship attractive. If you're a small-business owner, make sure you vet your potential team members before you become unequally yoked professionally.

The Right Strategy is Free

Now I'm going to go old school on you. Operating systems, podcasts, sales funnels, and technologies are tremendous, but there is no substitute for good old-fashioned relationship building. The right strategy is free; notice I didn't say easy. There will never be a time when relationship building won't be an essential element in executing your dream. When it's so noisy out there how do you establish true collaboration and not merely a digital connection? Out of all the speaking engagements I've had over the past two years, only one was the result of a "blind" submission, the rest were referrals, spin-offs, and repeats. Which isn't to say that I don't still comb the web for "request for speaker proposals", it just means that the best resource for filling my **Resources** pipeline are the ones I already have.

You're going to be tempted by countless specialists, experts, coaches, consultants, and salespeople who are going to call you and tell you that if you pay them X amount of dollars, they will make you X times famous. Please don't fall for this. I can't tell you how much money I threw away on web design, publicists, advertisers, #1 best seller rankings, and other pay-to-play schemes. The best way to find your revenue stream is through good old-fashioned grit and diligence. My father used to joke that whenever someone would call him and promise to solve all his problems for $10,000, he would say, *"Well if I pay you $10,000 that solves your problem, but what about mine?"* If you pay someone to have you ripen out of season, you'll never survive. Growth needs to be organic in order for it to produce a bountiful harvest. Even if you do get that big spike in business or opportunity, you won't be seasoned enough to sustain it.

Just look at Abraham and Sarah who tried to force the timing of God's promise. Both of them were well beyond child-bearing years but had been given a promise from God that Sarah would have a son. Rather than wait for God's timing, she enlisted Hagar, her Egyptian handmaid, to fulfill the promise. In Genesis 16 we see that Hagar gives birth to a son, Ishmael, but is told her son will live in conflict with his neighbors. Sarah then gave birth to Isaac; whose name means laughter or rejoicing. Remember that while we are waiting for God's **Resources**, rejoice and laugh while waiting in the midst of toil. If we try and shortcut God, we can be sure that any fruit we produce will be marred by conflict and war.

Nobody knows your message or your customers better than you, so don't outsource growth to someone who is not an **Advocate** for your organization. Growth can only come from within. Now, does this mean you shouldn't network or accept a friend's invitation to introduce you to a potential partner? No, it does not. What I am saying is do not pay someone to do this for you. If they are your true **Advocate** (see previous chapter) they will freely do this for you. I am not saying there won't be times when we do need to hire an outside expert, but more often than not, we hire them too soon and it is a waste of precious **Resources**. Make sure you've done all the grunt work and are clear in what you expect them to do. This due diligence and pre-work will save time, money, and heartache in the end.

> "God is more anxious to bestow His blessings
> on us than we are to receive them."
> —St. Augustine

The Inevitable Drought or "Show Me the Manna!"

What do you do when your **Resources** dry up? Quit? Complain? Soldier on? Like a stream going underground, sometimes prosperity goes out of sight. Make sure you don't move from miracles to murmurings. The quickest way to kill any chance at forward progress is to complain. That's why negativity cannot be tolerated in any form in any entity. A journey that should have taken the Israelites 11 days took 40 years because whining became their mission. By the grace of God, even in our most ungrateful, prideful states, He still provides for us. Check out Deuteronomy 8:4 where God gave them clothing that did not wear out and feet that did not swell or blister and again in Deuteronomy 29:5 where they wore shoes for forty years that did not wear out! There was also food (manna) divinely delivered every single day without fail and was all they needed to live.

Many times, we are given the tools to deal with our problems or to move forward, but we need to pick up what God is putting down! Many people go through life dead, long before they are buried. But thank God, He made us so we don't stink until we're put in the ground! Many people claim they are in their comfort zone, but actually, they are miserable. How do I know this? First, because we are made in the image of greatness. Just because you haven't claimed your inheritance doesn't mean it doesn't exist. A squirrel who refuses to climb trees and store acorns is still a squirrel. He just doesn't act like one. Second, because I can hear with my spiritual ear what people are really saying with their hearts and not their mouths. I look them right in the eyes and ask them if they are in their comfort zone, why are they so uncomfortable?

They are uncomfortable because we were created to live life and to live it abundantly thanks to the work of our Creator and Father.[7] Anything less than that is an abomination to nature— let alone ourselves and those around us. That's why there's an epidemic of addiction. When people deny, avoid, or rebuke their greatness, they need to numb or delude themselves. This only creates a great gap in their life. One of my book club participants told me that disease is actually being at "dis" "ease" with yourself. We need to dream big to be of service for the

Kingdom and that entails picking up the tools that God places in our lives.

Remember the Ravens and the Rains

Elijah is one of my favorite prophets in the Bible. In 1 Kings 17, this prophet of God drank out of a brook and was fed by ravens after declaring to evil King Ahab *"there will be neither dew nor rain in the next few years except at my word."* After announcing the great drought, God directed Elijah to travel and hide from Ahab in a ravine where he could drink from a brook of water and be fed by ravens. Elijah had to go into full-on baby bird mode while the ravens brought him bread and meat twice a day and he drank from the brook.

Sometime later the brook dried up because there was no rain in the land and Elijah was directed to the village of Zarephath where he met a widow. He asked her for a little water and bread to which the widow replied she only had enough for one last meal for her and her son before they died from starvation. Elijah told her to go ahead and bring the food and water, and her jars of oil and flour would never be empty until the Lord released rains into the land. God enacted a miracle true to Elijah's word.

Luke 12:24 also reminds us of the ravens stating, *"Consider the ravens: They do not sow or reap, they have no storeroom or barn; yet God feeds them. And how much more valuable you are than birds!"* When you are concerned or downright scared that you do not possess the means to finish the tasks at hand, I want you to remember the ravens. When the rains of prosperity are held back, God will still guide and direct your steps. He will also provide the daily **Resources** required. Remember the

Lord's Prayer? Give us this day our daily bread? We need to grasp at and cling to this concept.

Too many times we are worried about our 'end of quarter' bread, or our retirement bread. It takes the gift of faith to be content with living each day wholly dependent on the **Resources** delivered—literally in the case of Elijah—from above. And while the Bible does instruct us to store up **Resources** for times of famine[8], remember everything which comes into our grasp is God's anyways. We are merely stewards entrusted with putting his heavenly means to lasting earthly use.

The Blessing of Sharing Your Resources

At this very moment, you have something you no longer need that could infinitely bless someone else. Maybe it's an extra car that you no longer need, or maybe it's a closet full of clothes you no longer wear. I have the blessing of living in a large home and I've opened it up to young women who needed a place to stay. As a publisher, I have access to hundreds of free books which I donate to men in correctional facilities so they can continue to hone their minds and hearts.

The interesting thing about money is that the more you give away the more you have. In his book, *Life is Tremendous*, my father stated that one of the Laws of Leadership is "Give to Give." If you give to get, that's not giving; that's trading. They're all God's **Resources** anyway so don't be stingy. Think about the precious non-profits out there that rely on the literal kindness of strangers to fund their salaries and missional work. One of the greatest books I've read about the righteous use of wealth was *The Search for God and Guinness: A Biography of Beer that Changed the World.* Author Stephen Mansfield shares how Arthur Guinness was deeply influenced by John

Wesley's social teaching. John Wesley used to say, *"Make all you can, save all you can, give all you can,"* and that mantra gave the upper class and the merchant class a mission. Arthur Guinness began to think differently about how to use his wealth. He started the first Sunday schools in Ireland and founded hospitals for the poor; he positioned his company to transform lives. Don't decry wealth, it's what makes the mission bells ring and pays wages so people can provide a living.

My father taught me the more books he gave away for free the more books he sold. Sounds counterintuitive doesn't it? Not when you realize that generosity and kindness are not finite slices of the pie that need to be guarded. That type of thinking is a scarcity mentality and it's one of the biggest problems afflicting mankind. Cain killed Able because he thought God's favor directed toward his brother meant he would have less. This selfishness is at the root of all sibling rivalries, or any rivalry for that matter. Don't worry about lost **Resources**; it's all God's anyways and he will replenish them when and how he deems. Just look at Job who lost everything, loved ones, friends, health, and wealth, all because God allowed Satan to attempt to derail him. In the end God gave Job twice as much as he had before.[9]

Friends, I have had people sue, serve, depose, slander, and downright extort me for the hard-earned **Resources** God blessed me with. Make no mistake; He will have an accounting for this and will set everything right. There is no money tree; you've got to dig in and cultivate your own wealth. But there is also no limit to the amount of wealth in the universe so get out of the scarcity mentality. My father entrusted this business to me so I could continue to bless others with the **Resources** I had. The day I stop having the means to give is the day I close the business because on that day the Lord will have something else for me to do.

It's Not Rude to be Shrewd

Shrewd tends to have a negative connotation outside of the business arena. Everyone else tends to be quite naïve about how the world works. The definition of shrewd is having or showing a sharp power of judgment. Shrewdness is a clever resourcefulness in practical matters. Another name for shrewd is sagacious, which suggests wisdom and farsightedness.

I adore shrewd people because they are cautious optimists. They run any enterprise like a business and not like a charity. They are pragmatists with an understanding of people. They comprehend the way the world works in the here and now (not how the pie in the sky optimists think it should work) and negotiate towards a better future deal. I recently got married and this is one of the many tremendous traits that most attracted me to my spouse. He is savvy and shrewd. Hubba hubba!!

Shrewdness is not dishonesty; shrewdness is not cunning or deceit. There are many people out there that are on the take. I meet countless numbers of them in my industry alone. I'm sure you have as well. However, shrewd people know that action taken today will store up goodwill and favor in the future. Is that wrong? No! That's incredibly brilliant. Look at the parable of the crooked manager in Luke 16:1-13. This mangy manager was taking advantage of the resources of his wealthy business owner! Sounds familiar?? Yep, some things within human nature are timeless.

In this parable, just when the crooked manager was about to get fired, he went out to all the individuals who owed the wealthy man money and cut them a deal. That's right; he ingratiated himself to them by telling them to decrease what they owed by rewriting their bills. He did this presumably so when the inevitable pink slip came his way, he would have some friends to use as references or as new bosses or coworkers. In this way, they would be indebted to him, so he'd have a least some means of provision.

Jesus then commends this behavior, which, as an ethicist, always disturbed me. Isn't this fruit from the poisonous tree, and ill-gotten gain? How can this possibly be a "good" practice? Upon closer inspection, however, the point of this parable seems to be that a wise person understands that their season of strength, opportunity, and wealth is fleeting. Money comes and goes.

Sooner or later, we all run out of vitality, our prospects dim, and our wealth deserts us. Every person fades and eventually fails, but the wise man thinks about the future and orchestrates a plan. As much as we like to think we'll never die, every day that passes brings us one step closer to death. So be wise and use everything at your disposal to impact the world tremendously. That's why my father gave away books, books, and more books, and almost every dollar he made. He knew there would come a time when he would no longer be able to do so. Was it a wise business decision to give away costly goods for free and donate to organizations from which he got nothing financially? By worldly standards, no, but by eternal standards, you better believe it.

I'd like to think that this is one of the things my father taught me that I've continued since taking the helm. I think of all the people on the receiving end of his generosity daily and want to keep that tremendous legacy going. I understand that while I may never be counted among the most financially successful speakers of the 21st century, I will surely be counted as one of the shrewdest. Always remember that even if there is no financial benefit, your actions may be a considerable investment in eternity and that is authentic leadership at its finest.

Failing to Plan is Planning to Fail

I hope you've seen how important **Resources** are in sustaining the greatness within. People who start out on a journey without taking the time to prepare and pack are destined to get stranded by the wayside. Many of us start out with a bang, but finishing strong is extremely important. You don't want to take yourself or your team through a challenge unless you are optimistic you can turn it into an opportunity. We need to count the costs daily and make sure we have what is needed. Luke 14:28-30 puts it brilliantly:

> *"Suppose one of you wants to build a tower.*
> *Won't you first sit down and estimate the cost to see*
> *if you have enough money to complete it? For if you*
> *lay the foundation and are not able to finish it,*
> *everyone who sees it will ridicule you, saying,*
> *'This person began to build and wasn't able to finish.'"*

This is the reason why exemplary followers, who give you great insight into what is actually needed to make things happen and to work efficiently and judiciously with the **Resources** given, are essential. My professional experience has been that the smaller the team the more productive it is. I am a huge **Advocate** of the phrase 'lean and mean'. Bigger isn't always better. Bigger organizations tend to collect a great deal of bloat and bureaucracy. Smaller entities just can't survive with that type of drag. Make sure you jettison anything that might be weighing on you or slowing you down and only bring on board those people, processes, and pieces that are going to orient your trajectory forward and upward.

Money Does Makes the World Go Round

One last point about **Resources,** how you manage money is a huge part of this section. Money is not evil, however, the love of it is.[10] We must be careful to use money and not let it use us. Money allows me to do ministry and to win friends and influence people; to have a more tremendous life. Money allows me to bless others and for others to bless me. I run a for profit business, however, close to 90 percent of my activity (to include financial gifting) is done to support non-profits whose work I am delighted to be a part of. By doing so the corruption of money is redeemed as an investment in lives.

My earthly father set the business up with the sole intent to continue giving after he emigrated to Heaven. My Heavenly Father is not in a position of need and gives freely and abundantly, to include giving us His own Son so that we could spend eternity with Him. Money can be a heavenly investment and when you treat it as such you have the opportunity to use your income to honor God. Because honor begets honor, God will grant increase and blessings. Always remember, if we are faithful with the little things, we will be given even greater things.[11] So, make every dollar count!

Final Thoughts

Although we strive for the ideal, we live in the real; and that means we must have the tools at our disposal so we can put our dreams to work. One of the saddest things in the world is to see someone with the fire in their belly who does not have the means to get the job done. **Singularity, Persistence,** and **Advocates** are all vital pieces of the equation, but without the right **Resources,** you'll never be able to execute your plans.

Get clear on what's involved to get to the next level. Push off anything that isn't an immediate need. Research and network until you identify a person, program, or platform that will deliver the goods and remember, what works for someone else may not work for you. So, take your time to do your homework and define your scope of work. Once this is done, you can begin contracting out for help where you need it the most and don't forget to allow space for God to deliver the impossible. He's done it through all of history and He desires to do it for you too!

Onto **Knowledge!**

SPARK

FIVE

KNOWLEDGE: RECALIBRATE ON LEARNING

"You'll be the same person five years from now that you are today except for two things; the people you meet and the books you read."

—Charlie "Tremendous" Jones

"Leadership is lifelong learning."

—Tracey C. Jones

Do you suffer from indecisiveness—you want to make a decision but doubt your own ability to make the correct one? Do you let analysis paralysis cause you to miss opportunities and make you second guess yourself? This chapter is all about discovering how to build up your perceived self-efficacy which is your belief in your ability to make competent decisions. The beauty of learning is that you become less fearful of making mistakes because you know every decision—right or wrong—brings you closer to your desired goal. The answers are there; you've just got to find them, and you will.

No Growing Without Knowing

I was raised by a bookaholic. If there was one constant in my life growing up—it was books. But not just any books, personal development books. In fact, I think I read *How to Win*

Friends and Influence People before cracking open *The Pokey Little Puppy*. There's even a form of counseling known as Bibliotherapy which uses selected reading materials as thera-peutic aids in medicine and in psychiatry. My father was a big believer in the solution of personal problems through directed reading. Whenever someone would come to him with an issue or seeking input, he'd direct them into his vast library and tell them to select a book. Then he'd take a seat with them and have them begin reading aloud. Within fifteen to twenty minutes they would stop reading, look up at my father and exclaim, "How did you know that's exactly what I needed?" This happened every single time.

How and why this happened is no mystery. My father's life revolved around the people he met and the books he read. He made sure he had a steady diet of tremendousness every day of his earthly life. You see, he could look at someone and see if they had a reading deficiency. You can see it in their hollow eyes, furrowed brows, and listless lips. My father even encouraged us to read by paying us for book reports we would compose. We would agree on a title—usually one that was historical, spiritual, or character-building—then we would earn a specific agreed upon amount when our book report was submitted and reviewed.

My father shared this motivational tip in his book, *Life is Tremendous*, where he encouraged my brother Jere to earn money to buy a car when he turned sixteen by submitting book reports. He told him, *"If you read in style you'll drive in style; but if you read like a bum you'll drive like a bum."* Jere went on to read hundreds of books and wrote my father "Dear Dad" postcards with a life changing thought everyday he was away at college.

> *"My Best Friend is a person who will*
> *give me a book I have not read."*
> —*Abraham Lincoln*

Books are Your Best Friends

There's yet another type of efficacy called, intellectual or cognitive efficacy. Intellectual efficacy is measured in terms of perceived capability to perform everyday cognitive tasks and to learn new things. Mortimer Adler (n.d.) wrote, *"The purpose of learning is growth, and our minds, unlike our bodies, can continue growing as we continue to live."* Another term for intellectual efficacy is cognitive motivation, whereby people motivate themselves and guide their actions anticipatorily through the exercise of forethought. They anticipate likely outcomes of prospective actions, set goals for themselves, and plan courses of action designed to realize valued futures.[1]

The monthly book clubs I conduct in three Pennsylvania State Correctional Institutions have been going on for years. The attendees have read upwards of fifty books. Getting an inside look at the life of those behind bars has been a real eye-opening experience for me. There are programs for the men that teach them job-skills. They can earn degrees of higher education. All types of religious services take place every day of the week and there are classes upon classes for the men to learn and improve their life skills. The men told me that if you don't exit prison a better version of yourself, you've been killing time. I think how often those of us on the "outside" kill time. But the truth of the matter is, we don't kill time; time kills us. From the moment we are born our death clocks start. We have an undetermined amount of time on this planet in order to evolve into whatever we choose between our start and end dates.

One of my favorite quotes by Oswald Chambers is, *"We should always choose our books as God chooses our friends, just a bit beyond us, so that we have to do our level best to keep up with them."* Just like with everything else in life, we must be intentional about what we allow into our brains. If you pick up a book and realize it's just not doing it for you, or it's causing you to think things that are not edifying, put it down, and don't pick it up again. It's like walking away from a bad conversation or changing the channel when something unhealthy comes on the TV or computer screen.

One of the top comments I get after speaking is people thanking me for reigniting their desire and need to read. Their reception of this call to action lifts my spirit. I don't want you to just hear what I've learned; I want to turn you on to the endless source of potential propulsion, so you'll continue to soar to new heights. You just can't get to where you need to be without learning new things and unlearning old ones. Here is the top reason why you should read: *the more **Knowledge** you possess, the more peace you possess.* Truth.

Read to Live

We can't do anything about what we don't know and there's a whole lot we don't know! When I began my doctoral journey, many folks asked me why on earth I would go back to school at "this stage" of my life, as if I was doing this to gain something in some manner of transaction. I was always mystified whenever I would get this question. The answer is simple....I wanted to continue to learn; I wanted to transform, not just transact.

The greatest thing I learned from my doctoral program was the requirement to only reference grounded research from peer reviewed journals. When you cut out opinion, feelings, whining, ranting, and other forms of reptilian brain communication, life becomes so much quieter. It gives you time to think and to converse. Now, whenever someone tells me something to get a rise or response, I simply ask them to name their sources. *If you can't cite it don't write it.* Life's too short to cast pearls amongst swine. I only have so many brain cells and I do not want them occupied with falsehoods or vitriol. If the individual has sources such as blogs, websites, mainstream/social media, or late-night TV, end of conversation. You just can't imagine how much more productive time and how much less stress you have when you adopt this way of thinking and living.

All of us alive today have an unlimited amount of knowledge in the palms of our hands. Every time I come across an issue and I am uncertain how to best move forward (how to start a backpack leaf blower, how to help a gifted child focus on getting homework done, how to set healthy boundaries with siblings, you name it) I go online. Ambrose Bierce (1842-1914) said, *"There is nothing new under the sun but there are lots of old things we don't know."* We have access to the entire body of knowledge of the whole human race! The world is literally at your fingertips so let them do the walking and let your brain do the absorbing. The state of learning is an active one. I remember reading Mortimer Adler's, *How to Read a Book*, and weeping the entire way through it. I just could not get over the power of the written word and the gift we have been given by our Creator who gave us his mind.

Practicing Mind Control

Did you know that you can exhibit the superhero behavior of mind control without having to go through a spider bite, gamma radiation, or mutation? Romans 8:5-8 talks directly about this. Where do we set our minds? Where do we exhibit mind control? We must set our mind. If we don't actively set it, someone or something else will. I have learned some excellent tips on how to keep my mind as sharp as a tack so I can do battle and be victorious! First, I Sabbath. That means at least one day a week I turn off everything so I can be still and hear what is next.

If our electronic devices need to be restarted for updates and recharged for power, why do we think we can run our minds and bodies without the proper care and maintenance? I also ensure my space is clear of clutter and I do not have anything open on my computer that is not directly linked to the task at hand. Phones are turned off as is the music. You need quiet to hear what is about to be said. God's mercies are new every morning; therefore, it's up to us to learn how to recognize them in deeper and different ways.

I also take time to enjoy nature. I breathe in fresh air. I have three dogs that enjoy running trails. I adore gardening and physical labor. I work out at least three times a week. I take care of my shell because I need to run the race. I get eight hours of sleep a night. I used to need less, but find as I get older, I need more. I do not have a television in my bedroom. I do not watch television more than 30 minutes a day. I also have not touched sugar in years. That is the single most important thing I have ever done for my health. My mind is so much clearer and focused without the effects of sugar. The best part is, I don't even think about it. Yes, I could "reward" myself or "cheat" every now and then, but I don't because my brain tells me I no longer desire sugar.

The Desire to be Developed

In any organization, the need for each member to be developed is critical. Growth isn't just for the leaders, it's for everyone. During my doctoral research on the theory of motivation I asked my participants to rate their need to be developed. I wanted to see if the need to be developed translated to a higher level of confidence and effectiveness in meeting challenges. Several participants stated their desire to be developed decreased the older they got and the closer they got to retirement. They saw no benefit to continue completing additional schooling or pursuing advancement. While I understand the need to learn in order to climb the corporate ladder may decrease as the corporate ladder shrinks or disappears, I am talking about learning for the sake of being transformed and not for the sake of getting a higher title or salary. In top tier organizations, individuals at all levels and tenures should have a need for professional development so they can continue to pour into the organization.

In the military we had many clearances and you only had access to certain pieces of information if you had a *"need to know"*. I am talking about learning because you have *"a need to grow"*. There is also an incredible amount of research surrounding mental plasticity and the remarkable resiliency and retraining available in our brain. Mark Victor Hansen said, *"Read books, listen to audios, attend seminars—they are the decades of wisdom reduced to invaluable hours."*

As stated earlier, my father exposed me to the love of reading. Although he wasn't a "learned" man (he only made it through the 8th grade), he was respected globally for his wisdom and discernment. Although I was exposed to his love of books, I had not made this love my own conviction until I came back to run the business in January 2009. I figured if I was running a publishing company and was to carry on a legacy of tremendous books, I'd better get to reading!! The more I immersed myself in reading, the more my love for great books grew. So even if you don't naturally love to read, keep at it.

You can develop this skill just like any other. Philippians 4:8 states we are to think on these things that promote excellence, and that would most certainly be tremendous books.

Leaders are Readers

Earl Nightingale said that if you study one topic, one hour every work day for five years, you will become a national expert (1250 hours). So, for those of us who know we are not intellectually gifted, this should give great hope that we can become not only learned, but an expert in a field. That's what makes people valuable, what they know and what they can do. We can always make ourselves more valuable to our families, our friends, our relationships, our churches, and our jobs by becoming an expert.

If you recall back to the first section of the acronym **SPARK**, that's what **Knowledge** in pursuit of **Singularity** is all about. Pick that one thing and go to town. Dig for those nuggets of wisdom. Put on your researcher hat. You are in the realm of discovery. My father scanned hundreds of thousands of books in his lifetime but had his top 40 that he always went back to. Those were his foundational books from the seminal thinkers. Truth is timeless, however how it is contextualized is always changing. That's why it's important to digest a healthy diet of the old and the new. New knowledge has sprung from the existing body of knowledge. That is why people like me get a Ph.D.—to add one little kernel of knowledge to the existing universe of everything ever known to mankind. It's pretty amazing when you think about it.

Always keep a tablet or device nearby to write down what you thought as a result of what you read. Writing while listening or reading enables retention. Some studies say it even increases learning by 100 percent. When I speak at an event, I can tell the people who are there to learn. They are actively listening and writing things down. They are taking notes and screen shots of my slides with their cameras. They will go back to their rooms that night to take more notes and digest what they heard so they can begin application as soon as possible.

According to Beesley and Apthorp's meta-analysis in 2010, showing students how to take effective notes is strongly correlated with better achievement. One study from 20 years ago (when computer notes would have been an unaffordable oddity) tested college students to see if taking notes supported retention of factual **Knowledge**.[2] It did: the note-taking group scored better than a group who took no notes during the lecture, but later wrote essays about what they'd learned. The note-taking group also outscored a control group who reviewed the material but did no writing at all. *In short, we're more apt to remember words and content we take notes on.*

Mind Renewal Ancora Imparo

My life verse is Romans 12:2 where Paul states, *"Do not conform to the pattern of this world but be transformed by the renewing of your mind. Then you will be able to test and approve what God's will is—his good, pleasing and perfect will"*. Paul's letter to the Romans included practical teaching on how to live a godly life and reminded his followers that mental rejuvenation is the key. You cannot live a tremendous life without tremendous reading and learning habits. The two are inextricably linked. Show me your relationship with learning and I'll show you your relationship with life. My father wasn't **Tremendous** because of who he was, but because he was in a constant state of regeneration, moving from person to person like a prophet, putting books in their hands and extolling them to read in order to live.

Life is all about motivation. George et al. states, *"Intrinsic motivations are congruent with your values and are more fulfilling than extrinsic motivations"*. I had heard this early in life but never fully understood it. There comes a time when you stop just taking it in and begin flowing it back out. When people would ask me if my father was always so efficacious, I would say yes. He had to allow what he was taking in to flow out otherwise he would burst at the seams! So many people walk around completely drained, expecting others to fill them up. Life can only be lived from the inside out. Self-awareness is challenging and draining. Without the ability to consciously review what is transpiring and stay attentive to the Holy Spirit, you'll run out of steam. That's why staying in the scriptures and great books are critical. Your supply lines will dry up if you don't. No one is smart enough to figure it out on their own, nor are we intended to neglect the brilliant wisdom and hard-fought **Knowledge** earned by our predecessors.

At the age of 87, in the year 1562, Michelangelo, the largely self-taught Italian sculptor, painter, architect and poet proclaimed *"Ancora imparo"*, which is Italian for *"I am still learning"*.

Pablo Casals was a brilliant cellist, and I love a remark he reportedly made when he was in his eighties or nineties. He continued to practice intensely with his cello in those golden years, and when he was asked why he was so diligent he replied with one of these statements: *"I think I'm making progress. I think I see some improvement."* You see, none of us ever truly arrives until we get to the other side. While we're on earth it's our job to continue to become the best version of ourselves and this includes, first and foremost, our minds. The greatest motivation you can ever possess, is the desire to learn. Once you have that, you have everything you need to ignite, and reignite for life, the greatness within.

Life-Changing Classics

One of the most frequent excuses people use for not reading is the lack of time. I know those of you reading this book would never say that, but I am keenly aware of the demands of each day. It takes a great deal of work and we need to be good stewards of our time! As a publisher, I work to create content that a busy person can read on a flight leg from DC to O'Hare. I learned the power of condensed content from my father who created a series of booklets titled **Life-Changing Classics**. At the time of this book there are 32 in the series and we produce new ones every year. These are quick but powerful reads that cover some of the greatest individuals and concepts of all time. A complete list of the series is in the back of this book.

People love these **Life-Changing Classics** because they contain the wisdom of the ages, they can change lives, and especially because they can be read in one sitting. Reading these tremendous treasures is not just about the act of reading; but the results of thinking. Beautiful sacred jewels pop up out of pages from people who have long since departed this life. People also love them because they can hand them out to clients, friends, co-workers, and family. My father told me to never give someone my business card because it would just get thrown away (sometimes even before I had left the room!). Give them a book instead because they will never throw away a book—especially one that is signed with a personal note! He was right. We have businesses, churches, and groups order these booklets by the tens of thousands to give away at events or as a Thank You.

Cultivating a Love of Learning

When I first moved back home to pick up my father's tremendous mantle, I knew I had to cultivate a love of reading. I read one of the **Life-Changing Classics**, *Books are Tremendous*, and saw for the first time that books really are tremendous! My point is this; you can cultivate a love of reading. Some of us are born with it; others need to develop it. Just like being a natural at sports or music, some of us are coded as readers in the womb. But just like every other skill in life, reading can be developed. During my doctoral program we read a book by Mortimer Adler titled, *How to Read a Book*. As mentioned earlier, I was absolutely gob smacked! I thought reading was a passive experience that you picked up when you felt like it. Boy was I wrong! If you really want a great book on how to truly get the most out of every book you read, I highly recommend Mr. Adler's classic.

Always remember, you can cultivate a love of learning. You need to work at it like anything else in life. **Knowledge** isn't about learning or unlearning; it's about spiritual discernment and growing in wisdom. Second Timothy 2:15 states, *"Do your best to present yourself to God as one approved, a worker who does not need to be ashamed and who correctly handles the word of truth."*

Final Thoughts

We all have a brain, but do we have a mind to use it? Not just any mind, but the mind of Christ? The human brain is the most unbelievable piece of machinery in the universe. We are called to grow in grace and the knowledge of God. We have the wisdom of the ages passed down to us through millennia of books. We have the living breathing word of God delivered to us in the Bible and neuroscience telling us our brains can be retrained. Learning truly never stops and leadership is lifelong learning.

Are we infusing our need to be developed? Or have we gotten comfortable in our level of success or perhaps feel we are too mature or accomplished to be expected to learn new tricks. Or are we falling deeper in love with learning every day? Do we have a collection of books that we look at with love in our eyes and hearts because we know how they have transformed us? There is always room to improve; there is always room to learn; there is always room for more greatness in your life. Make sure a steady diet of reading is included in your daily routine and watch your brain begin to grow!

FINAL EXHORTATION

Whenever we have an appliance or an automobile that doesn't work what's the first thing we check? The battery or the plug. Why? Because without a source of power, nothing works. So, what's your source of power? You can read all the books in the world and fill your head with every imaginable tactic to get yourself organized and in the know, however, without your ignition source, you'll fail to turn over.

As you've read in this book, we need *Confidence* (manifested through **Singularity** and **Persistence**) and *Competency* (exhibited through **Advocates, Resources,** and **Knowledge**). But the final key to igniting all that is within you is to *Care*. No one can *care* for you; you need to care enough to stop doing what you're doing and commit to taking a different path. This must be innate within you. If you don't care enough to make a positive change in your life, no amount of catchy acronyms, or mental hooks will provide your fuel to live a tremendous life. When you care you prioritize. When you care you take ownership. When you care you begin doing research to cure your ignorance. When you care you begin looking for the right kind of people in your life. When you care you find the **Resources** you need and put them to use. One of the most heart-breaking things in life is to watch people live in pain or self-doubt, unwilling to take the actions needed to cure themselves. The great thing about being a human being is that we all have free will.

The Potential Principle

One of my favorite reads is a book by Edwin Louis Cole titled, *The Potential Principle*. Cole references the feeding of the 5,000 in the Gospels and brings out an incredible point. It wasn't until the disciples placed the baskets with the loaves and fishes in our Lord's hands that the miracle happened. What an incredible insight for us. We can live life superabundantly. But the work must come from you; not to you, not for you, but from you. That work entails doing our part, but also putting everything—and I mean everything—squarely in His hands. So, if you are ready to partner with God, I want you to claim Ephesians 3:20 and get ready to ignite the greatness within; *"Now to him who is able to do immeasurably more than all we ask or imagine, according to his power that is at work within us."* We are nothing without him, and we are everything to him. That is why we have greatness within.

In 1 Corinthians 3:6-7, the Apostle Paul states, *"I planted the seed, Apollos watered it, but God has been making it grow. So, neither the one who plants nor the one who waters is anything, but only God, who makes things grow."* You've got to have the seeds of desire. Behavior changes when you possess two things; first a reasonable expectation of success; and second a desire to change. Then, and only then, when we focus on the work, the journey, the growth, does God bestow the outcome. Thank God we don't have to worry about that and are free to focus on the delivery.

In 2 Peter 1:4, Peter says, *"Through these he has given us his very great and precious promises, so that through them you may participate in the divine nature, having escaped the corruption in the world caused by evil desires."* The world is going to literal hell in a hand basket. We not only have an escape option; we also have a tremendous solution to create heaven on earth right here and right now.

All we are responsible for now is passing on the mantle of glorification. To do that, we must first ignite the glory of God within us. What good is an inheritance if you don't show up to claim it and enjoy its transformative power in your life? Perhaps you have come to the end of this book full of contemplation and are now officially ready to dial it in.

There is a passage in John 17 that succinctly summarizes everything you're ever going to need to do in life. In this passage, Jesus prays for himself. He prays to God to glorify the Son so that the Son may glorify him. But He doesn't stop just there. In verses 6 through 9 he prays for his disciples and his prayer follows the same steps outlined in this book.

Singularity - *Seeing* (verse 6): *"They were yours; you gave them to me."* The disciples were given to Christ by God for a **singular** purpose.

Persistence - *Working* (verse 6): *"and they have obeyed your word."* The disciples forsook everything in their desire to follow the instruction and commandments of Jesus. They **persisted**.

Advocates - *Receiving* (verse 7): *"Now they know that everything you have given me comes from you."* The disciples know that everything comes from the ultimate **Advocate**, the Son of God.

Resources - *Using* (verse 8): *"For I gave them the words you gave me and they accepted them. They knew with certainty that I came from you, and they believed that you sent me."* The disciples were willing to accept the **Resources**, the words, the affirmation, that Jesus gave to them.

Knowledge - *Knowing* (verse 9): "*I pray for them. I am not praying for the world, but for those you have given me, for they are yours.*" The disciples knew with certainty that he came from God and believed. They were infused by the prayers of the Master for them. This was all the affirmation and certainty they needed.

Now that you have the tools to ignite the greatness within, I want you to claim it; to name it; to love it; to live it; and, most importantly, to share it. Because once you've got this five-step program dialed in, you'll want to share it with others so they can ignite their inner greatness as well. Here's to making the world a more tremendous place. Thank you so much for going on this journey with me. Be blessed and I look forward to changing the world with you!!

ENDNOTES

Author's Note

1. Cepeda & Martin (2005)

Introduction

1. Hannah et al., 2008
2. Zimmerman & Cleary, 2006
3. Pintrich & Schunk, 2002
4. Zimmerman & Cleary, 2006
5. Zimmerman & Cleary, 2006
6. Pintrich & Schunk, 2002
7. Schunk, 1983; Zimmerman & Paulsen, 1995
8. Zimmerman, 2000
9. Bandura, 1989, Page 733
10. McAdams, 2015
11. Bandura, 1986
12. Bandura, 1989
13. Bandura, 1988; Lazarus & Folkman, 1984; Meichenbaum, 1984; Sarason, 1975
14. Bandura, 1986;1989
15. Bandura, 1989, Page 732
16. Merzenich, Vleet, & Nahum, 2014
17. Green & Bavelier, 2008
18. Swain & Thompson, 1993; Merzenich, 2001, 2013; Weinberger, 2004; Gilbert et al., 2009
19. Merzenich, 2001, 2013
20. Dubrin, 2013
21. Merzenich et al., 2014

Chapter One – Spark: Singularity

1. Cloud, Safe People pg. 88
2. Prov. 29:18
3. Brown & Treviño, 2009; Edwards & Cable, 2009
4. Brown & Treviño, 2009

Chapter Two – Spark: Persistence

1. McAdams, 2015
2. James 1:2
3. 1 Kings 19:11-13
4. 2 Cor. 12:9-11

Chapter Three – Spark: Advocates

1. Gen. 2:18
2. 1 Pet. 5:8
3. Matt. 7:6
4. Matt. 17:1-2
5. Matt. 26:36-46
6. Ex. 14:13-14
7. 1 Cor. 4:16-17
8. John 6:68

Chapter Four – Spark: Resources

1. Eden, 2001, pg. 10
2. Eden, 2001; Eden & Sulimani, 2002
3. Goldstein, 2007
4. Dansereau, Graen, & Haga, 1975
5. Lambert, 2006
6. Dansereau, Graen, & Haga, 1975
7. John 10:10
8. Gen. 41:36
9. Job 42:10

10. 1 Tim 6:10
11. Luke 16:10

Chapter Five – Spark: Knowledge

1. Bandura, 1989
2. Beeson, 1996

SOURCES

Adler, M. J. (n.d.). *Mortimer J. Adler quotes*. Retrieved from http://www. quoteland.com/author/Mortimer-J-Adler-Quotes/2601/

Amodio, D. M., & Showers, C. J. (2005). 'Similarity breeds liking' revisited: The moderating role of commitment. *Journal of Social and Personal Relationships, 22*(6), 817–836. doi:10.1177/0265407505058701

Bandura, A. (1986). *Social foundations of thought and action: A social cognitive theory*. Englewood Cliffs, NJ: Prentice Hall.

Bandura, A. (1989). Regulation of cognitive processes through perceived self-efficacy. *Developmental Psychology, 25*(5), 729–735. doi:10.1037//0012-1649.25.5.729

Beesley, A. D., & Apthorp, H. S. (2010). Classroom Instruction That Works, Second Edition: Research Report. *Mid-Continent Research for Education and Learning (McREL)*.

Beeson, S. A. (1996). The Effect of Writing After Reading on College Nursing Students Factual Knowledge and Synthesis of Knowledge. *Journal of Nursing Education, 35*(6), 258–263. doi: 10.3928/0148-4834-19960901-06

Brown, M. E., & Treviño, L. K. (2006). Ethical leadership: A review and future directions. *The Leadership Quarterly, 17*(6), 595–616. doi:10.1016/j.leaqua.2006.10.004

Carlyle, T. (1840). *On heroes, hero-worship, and the heroic in history*. London, England: Chapman and Hall.

Cepeda, G., & Martin, D. (2005). A review of case studies publishing in management decision 2003–2004. *Management Decision, 43*(6), 851–876. doi:10.1108/00251740510603600

Cloud, H., & Townsend, J. S. (2016). *Safe people: how to find relationships that are good for you and avoid those that aren't*. Grand Rapids, MI: Zondervan.

Dansereau, F., Graen, G., &Haga, W. J. (1975). A vertical dyad linkage approach to leadership within formal organizations: A longitudinal investigation of the role making process. *Organizational Behavior and Human Performance, 13*(1), 46–78. doi:10.1016/0030-5073(75)90005-7

DuBrin, A. J. (2013). *Handbook of research on crisis leadership in organizations*. Cheltenham, UK: Edward Elgar.

Eden, D. (2001). Means efficacy: External sources of general and specific subjective efficacy. In M. Erez, U. Kleinbeck, & H. Thierry (Eds.), *Work motivation in the context of a globalizing economy* (pp. 65–77). Mahwah, NJ: L. Erlbaum Associates.

Eden, D., &Sulimani, R. (2002). Pygmalion training made effective: Greater mastery through augmentation of self-efficacy and means efficacy. In B. J. Avolio & F. J. Yammarino (Eds.), *Transformational and charismatic leadership: The road ahead* (pp. 287–308). Oxford, UK: Elsevier.

Edwards, J. R., & Cable, D. M. (2009). The value of value congruence. *The Journal of Applied Psychology, 94*(3), 654–677. doi:10.1037/a0014891

Erdoğan, B., Kraimer, M. L. and Liden, R. C. (2004). Work value congruence and intrinsic career success: The compensatory roles of leader-member exchange and perceived organizational support. *Personnel Psychology, 57*(2), 305–332. doi:10.1111/j.1744-6570.2004.tb02493.x

George, B., Sims, P., McLean, A. N., & Mayer, D. (2007). Discovering Your Authentic Leadership. Harvard Business Review, 85(2), 129-138

Gilbert, R., Widom, C. S., Browne, K., Fergusson, D. M., Elspeth, W., & Janson, S. (2009). Child Maltreatment 1: Burden and consequences of child maltreatment in high-income countries. *The Lancet, 373*(9657), 68–81. doi:10.1016/s0140-6736(08)61706-7

Goldstein J.A. (2007). A new model for emergence and its leadership implications. In J. K. Hazy, J. A. Goldstein & B. B. Lichtenstein (Eds.), *Complex systems leadership theory: New perspectives from complexity science on social and organizational effectiveness* (pp. 61–92). Mansfield, MA: Institute for the Study of Coherence and Emergence.

Green, C. S., & Bavelier, D. (2008). Exercising your brain: A review of human brain plasticity and training-induced learning. *Psychology and Aging, 23*(4), 692–701. doi:10.1037/a0014345

Hannah, S. T., Avolio, B. J., Luthans, F., & Harms, P. (2008). Leadership efficacy: Review and future directions. *The Leadership Quarterly, 19*(6), 669–692. doi:10.1016/j.leaqua.2008.09.007

Kelley, R. E. (1992). *The power of followership*. New York, NY: Currency Doubleday.

Kotter, J. P. (2010). *Leading change: Why transformation efforts fail*. Boston, MA: Harvard Business Press.

Lambert, S. J. (2006). Both art and science: Employing organizational documentation in workplace based research. In M. Pitt-Catauphes, E. E. Kossek, & S. Sweet (Eds.), *The work and family handbook: Multi-Disciplinary perspectives, methods and approaches* (pp. 503–525). Mahwah, NJ: Lawrence Erlbaum Associates.

McAdams, D. P. (2015). *Art and science of personality development.* New York, NY: Guilford.

Merzenich, M. M. (2001). Cortical plasticity contributing to child development. In J. McClelland & R. Siegler (Eds.), *Mechanisms in cognitive development* (pp. 67–96). Mahwah, NJ: Erlbaum.

Merzenich, M. M. (2013). *Soft-Wired: How the new science of brain plasticity can change your life.* San Francisco, CA: Parnassus Publishing.

Merzenich, M. M., Vleet, T. M., & Nahum, M. (2014). Brain plasticity-based therapeutics. *Frontiers in Human Neuroscience, 8.* doi:10.3389/fnhum.2014.00385

Pintrich, P. R., & Schunk, D. H. (2002). *Motivation in education: Theory, research, and applications* (2nd ed.). Upper Saddle River, NJ: Prentice Hall.

Rokeach, M. (1968). A theory of organization and change within value-attitude systems. *Journal of Social Issues, 24*(1), 13–33. doi:10.1111/j.1540-4560.1968.tb01466.x

Schunk, D. H. (1983). Progress self-monitoring: Effects on children's self-efficacyand achievement. *Journal of Experimental Education, 51*(2), 89–93. doi:10.1080/00220973.1982.11011845

Staff, F. C. (2012, September 20). *Change or Die. Retrieved from* https://www.fastcompany.com/52717/change-or-die

Suar, D., & Khuntia, R. (2010). Influence of personal values and value Congruence on Unethical Practices and Work Behavior. *Journal of Business Ethics, 97*(3), 443–460. doi:10.1007/s10551-010-0517-y

Swain, R. A., & Thompson, R. F. (1993). In search of engrams. In F. M. Crinella& J. Yu (Eds.), *Annals of the New York Academy of Sciences: Vol. 702. Brain mechanisms: Papers in memory of Robert Thompson* (pp. 27–39). New York, NY: New York Academy of Sciences.

Weinberger, N. M. (2004). Specific long-term memory traces in primary auditory cortex. *Nature Reviews Neuroscience, 5*(4), 279–290. doi:10.1038/nrn1366

Zhang, J., & Bloemer, J. (2011). Impact of value congruence on affective commitment: Examining the moderating effects. *Journal of Service Management, 22*(2), 160–182. doi: 10.1108/09564231111124208

Zimmerman, B. J. (2000). Self-Efficacy: An essential motive to learn. *Contemporary Educational Psychology, 25*(1), 82–91. doi:10.1006/ceps.1999.1016

Zimmerman, B. J., & Cleary, T. J. (2006). Adolescents' development of personal agency: The role of self-efficacy beliefs and self-regulatory skill. In F. Pajares & T. Urdan (Eds.), *Self-Efficacy beliefs of adolescents* (pp. 45–71). Information Age Publishing.

Zimmerman, B. J., & Paulsen, A. S. (1995). Self-monitoring during collegiate studying: An invaluable tool for academic self-regulation. *New Directions for Teaching and Learning, 1995*(63), 13–27. doi:10.1002/tl.37219956305

Short, impactful reads from the
Life-Changing Classics Series
Available at www.TremendousLeadership.com

3 Therapies of Life (The), by Charlie "Tremendous" Jones; Foreword by Dr. Tracey C. Jones.

7 Golden Rules of Milton Hershey (The), by Greg Rothman; Foreword by Richard Zimmerman.

7 Leadership Virtues of Joan of Arc (The), by Peter Darcy.

Acres of Diamonds, by Russell H. Conwell; Appreciation by John Wanamaker.

Advantages of Poverty, by Andrew Carnegie; Foreword by Dale Carnegie.

As a Man Thinketh, by James Allen.

Books Are Tremendous, edited by Charlie "T" Jones; Introduction by J.C. Penney.

"Bradford, You're Fired!", by William W. Woodbridge.

Breakthrough Speaking, by Mark Sanborn.

Character Building, by Booker T. Washington.

Discipleship, by John M. Segal

From Belfast to Narnia: The Life and Faith of C.S. Lewis, by The C.S. Lewis Institute.

Greatest Thing in the World (The), by Henry Drummond; Introduction by Dwight L. Moody.

Key to Excellence (The), by Charlie "T" Jones.

Kingship of Self-Control (The), by William George Jordan; Foreword by Charlie "T" Jones.

Lincoln Ideals (The), edited by Charlie "T" Jones.

Luther on Leadership, by Stephen J. Nichols.

Maxims of Life & Business, by John Wanamaker; Forewords by Elbert Hubbard and Russell Conwell.

Message to Garcia (A), by Elbert Hubbard.

My Conversion, by Charles Spurgeon; Edited & Compiled by Charlie "T" Jones.

Mystery of Self-Motivation (The), by Charlie "T" Jones.

New Common Denominator of Success (The), by Albert E.N. Gray; Foreword by Charlie "T" Jones.

Price of Leadership (The), by Charlie "T" Jones; foreword by Dr. Tracey C. Jones.

Reason Why (The), by R.A. Laidlaw; Introduction by Marjorie Blanchard.

Ronald Wilson Reagan: The Great Communicator, by Greg Rothman.

Self-Improvement through Public Speaking, by Orison Swett Marden; Introduction by Forrest Wallace Cato.

Science of Getting Rich: Abridged Edition (The), by Wallace D. Wattles; edited by Charlie "T" Jones.

Succeeding With What You Have, by Charles Schwab; Foreword by Andrew Carnegie.

That Something, by William W. Woodbridge; Introduction by Paul J. Meyer.

Three Decisions (The), by Charlie "T" Jones; Foreword by Dr. Tracey C. Jones.

Walt Disney: Dreams Really Do Come True!, by Jason Liller.

Wit and Wisdom of General George S. Patton (The), compiled by Charlie "T" Jones.

MORE RECOMMENDED READING

A Message to Millennials by Dr. Tracey C. Jones

Aligning Strategy and Sales: The Choices, Systems, and Behaviors that Drive Effective Selling by Frank V. Cespedes

Boundaries: When to Say Yes, How to Say No to Take Control of Your Life by Dr. Henry Cloud and Dr. John Townsend

The E-Myth Revisited by Michael Gerber

How to Read a Book by Mortimer Adler

Hung by the Tongue by Francis P. Martin

Life is Tremendous by Charlie "T" Jones

Man's Search for Meaning by Viktor Frankl

Maxims of Life & Business with Selected Prayers: Life-Changing Classics, Volume VII by John Wanamaker

My Utmost for His Highest by Oswald Chambers

The New Common Denominator of Success: Laws of Leadership, Volume IX by Albert E.N. Grey

The Potential Principle by Edwin Louis Cole

The Power of Followership by Robert Kelley

The Power of the Other: The Startling Effect Other People Have on You, from the Boardroom to the Bedroom and Beyond-and What to Do About It by Dr. Henry Cloud

Safe People: How to Find Relationships That Are Good For You and Avoid Those That Aren't by Dr. Henry Cloud and Dr. John Townsend

Shade of His Hand by Oswald Chambers

The Sales Messenger by MaryAnne Whibey-Davis

The Search for God and Guinness by Stephen Mansfield

Talking with God by François Fénelon

Think and Grow Rich by Napoleon Hill

The Three Decisions: Life-Changing Classics, Volume XV by Charlie "T" Jones

The Wit & Wisdom of General George S. Patton: Laws of Leadership Series, Volume VI Compiled by Charlie "T" Jones

ABOUT THE AUTHOR

Author, speaker, veteran, and international leadership expert, Dr. Tracey C. Jones is the President of Tremendous Leadership. She picked up the reigns from her father, Charlie "Tremendous" Jones in 2008. Tracey is a passionate lifelong learner and her career spans top positions in four major industries from the military to high tech to defense contracting and publishing. She is a graduate of the United States Air Force Academy, a decorated veteran who served in the First Gulf War and Bosnian War, earned an MBA in Global Management, and a Ph.D. in Leadership Studies through Lancaster Bible College. Tracey is also a faculty member of the prestigious Institute for Organization Management (IOM) and was awarded a Doctor of Humane Letters (honorary Ph.D.) from Central Penn College in 2017.

Tracey is the author of ten titles, five of which are children's books which use her rescue pets to teach character development to our next generation of emerging leaders. Tremendous Leadership funds a trust which has donated over $3.8M to local homeless shelters, recovery outreach and mission groups, disaster recovery organizations, and scholarships to local colleges in the past ten years. She is and has served on numerous non-profit boards where she uses her resources to spark the greatness in others. You can find her traveling the world speaking to groups spanning from women's ministries in Africa, to teaching middle schoolers in Europe. Tracey is married to a tremendous man, Mike, and enjoys the outdoors, biking, traveling, spending time with her pack of rescue pets, and giving others the tools to live a tremendous life.

MORE INFORMATION ON
DR. TRACEY JONES

SPEAKING

Many keynote speakers can be entertaining, but Tracey brings a unique approach to motivation that includes a call to action, complete with tools you can put to immediate use. Tracey is able to address the root issue that needs targeted, and jump-start the transformation needed to become tremendous. With Tracey's peer-reviewed research and her lifelong pursuit of learning, she is always looking for opportunities to help businesses with Continuing Education Credits, personality assessments, and actionable changes to invest value into their employees.

For more information on Tracey's speaking, visit
www.TraceyCJones.com

CONSULTATION

Merging organizations is easy; merging people is hard. Everyone processes change differently. As leaders, you can plan to avoid many things, but oftentimes companies spend 95% of efforts leading up to a merger on the financial aspects, and only 5% on human capital. The success of your merger will come from the perspective and personalities of your participants. Tracey can help you discover which employees are capable of being developed into co-leaders so you can press forward and uncover other potential problem areas, saving lost time, money, and resources. When it comes to a merger or acquisition, the best defense is a good offense.

Find out more about merger/acquisition consultation at
www.TraceyCJones.com/consultation

Books

Tremendous Leadership was established in the 60's to bring impactful reading to change the lives of working people. Not only can you find books of excellent caliber at TremendousLeadership.com, but the Tremendous Leadership team works as a third party distributor for many businesses who invest in their employees through the power of reading, offering titles from other publishers at bulk discounts to give away or sell at conferences, seminars, recognition ceremonies, in-house libraries, or as 'thank you's for your customers.

Contact us about our Tremendous titles at
www.TremendousLeadership.com

Podcast

Leadership is Learning. Listen as Dr. Tracey Jones brings her signature wit to discussions focusing on leadership typologies, styles, strategies, and of course, how to apply them today. As her father, Charlie "Tremendous" Jones said best, "You will be the same person in five years as you are today except for two things; the people you meet and the books you read." Check out the Tremendous Leadership podcast with Dr. Tracey Jones on youtube, itunes, spotify, and wherever you listen to podcasts.